FACULTY AND THE LIBRARY: THE UNDERGRADUATE EXPERIENCE

Larry Hardesty

Director of Library Services
Eckerd College
St. Petersburg, FL

ABLEX PUBLISHING CORPORATION
NORWOOD, NEW JERSEY 07648

027.7
H 218 F

Printed in the United States of America.

Library of Congress Cataloging-in-Publication Data

Hardesty, Larry L.
  Faculty and the library : the undergraduate experience / by Larry Hardesty.
    p.   cm.
  Includes bibliographical references and index.
  ISBN 0-89391-685-4
  1. Libraries, University and college—Relations with faculty and curriculum.   2. Libraries, University and college—Undergraduate libraries.   3. College teachers—Attitudes.   I. Title.
  Z675.U5H24   1990
  027.7—dc20   90-42434
                                                              CIP

Ablex Publishing Corporation
355 Chestnut Street
Norwood, New Jersey 07648

$ 37.50

TABLE OF CONTENTS

LIST OF TABLES

ABOUT THE AUTHOR

Larry Hardesty is director of library services at Eckerd College, St. Petersburg, Florida. He has a Ph.D. in library and information science from Indiana University, an M.A.L.S. from the University of Wisconsin-Madison, and additional graduate degrees in history and instructional development. He directed two library use instruction projects funded by the Council on Library Resources and served as a consultant for the Association of Research Libraries, Office of Management Studies. He authored *Slide/Tapes in Academic Libraries* (Jeffrey Norton, 1978), and co-compiled *User Instruction in Academic Libraries: A Century of Selected Readings* (with John P. Schmitt and John Mark Tucker) (Scarecrow,1986), *Mission Statements for College Libraries* (with Jamie Hastreiter and David Henderson) (ACRL, 1985), and *Periodicals in College Libraries* (with Jamie Hastreiter and David Henderson) (ACRL, 1987). His articles have appeared in *College & Research Libraries, Journal of Academic Librarianship, Library Research, Drexel Library Quarterly, Collection Management, Serials Librarian, Journal of Library Administration, Collection Building,* and *Library Scene.* He has authored chapters in various books and addressed national, regional, and local audiences on such topics as bibliographic instruction, college library standards, library evaluation, and college library administration. He is past president of the Florida chapter of the Association of College and Research Libraries and past secretary of the College Libraries Section of the Association of College and Research Libraries. Currently, he is a member of the board of directors of the Association of College and Research Libraries and of the Florida Library Association. He is on the editorial board and is the book review editor of *Collection Management.* He is also on the editorial board of *College & Research Libraries.*

PREFACE

What do faculty members think about the undergraduate educational role of the academic library? We entered the library profession in the early 1970s as academic librarians rediscovered bibliographic instruction. We found our responsibilities as a reference librarian exciting and challenging but also troubling. We soon concluded that most students made little or no use of the library and many of those who did barely tapped its potential. We quickly concluded that faculty members held the key to student library use.

We thought if only we would talk to faculty members about their assignments they might require students to use the library. Perhaps the faculty members might even invite us into the classroom to teach students how to use the library with some sophistication. Some, of course, did respond to our requests. We found their responses, however, far from reassuring.

Many faculty members did not want to give up class time for bibliographic instruction. Some faculty members thought undergraduates mastered (or should have mastered) how to use the library in high school or freshman English. They found no other guidance necessary. Others seemed content with library skills developed from high school reports—often uncritical compilation of information. Still others gave us a receptive audience. Nevertheless, they often did not seem to understand either the need or the means to involve undergraduates in the library.

We clearly remember the responses of two English professors to our conversations about freshman English library assignments. One asserted his students did not need instruction on how to use the library. He declared most of his students were going to graduate school. They could wait until then to learn how to use the library. Later the same day, his colleague declared most of his students were not going to graduate school. Therefore, they would not need instructions on how to use the library. Obviously, their responses puzzled and dismayed us.

Our examinations of circulation records provided additional disquieting information. Most undergraduates seldom checked any books out of the library. Many books remain uncirculated. Harvie Branscomb, Patricia

Knapp, and Evan Farber provided us with some insight into faculty members' views of the library. Nevertheless, we found few empirical investigations in this area. Finally, our doctoral dissertation provided the opportunity for us to examine more carefully the issue.

We base this book largely on our dissertation study conducted in the fall of 1981 and the spring of 1982. The text, however, has evolved over the years and we have expanded it with more recent research. For some parts we have borrowed heavily from our earlier publications. The early chapters provide the rationale and foundation for the study. The middle chapters discuss the faculty members' library attitudes in relation to various factors. The latter chapters give an overview of faculty culture and tell how to work with faculty members. The final chapter consists of a summary of our conclusions and recommendations. The appendices include a copy of the attitude scale we developed and a discussion of its psychometric characteristics. Through this information we have tried to provide a publication useful both to the practicing librarian and to the researcher in understanding what faculty members think about the undergraduate educational role of the academic library.

Larry Hardesty
St. Petersburg, Florida
September 25, 1989

ACKNOWLEDGMENTS

Many people made significant contributions toward the completion of this book. Literally hundreds of individuals shared their thoughts and time with me through lengthy interviews or the completion of the attitude scale. They are, of course, too many to name but I appreciate their help no less.

In particular, I thank Jim Martindale, director of libraries (retired) at DePauw University. Without his encouragement and cooperation, I would never have written this book. He allowed me the time and the flexibility to conduct much of the research for it in the midst of my other responsibilities. I thank Dr. David Kaser, chair of my dissertation committee and distinguished professor of library and information science at Indiana University. His infectious optimism, generosity with time, and sage advice immensely contributed to the completion of my dissertation. I also thank the other members of the dissertation committee at Indiana University (Professor Clayton Shepherd, Dr. Marcy Murphy, Dr. Tom Schwen, and Dr. David Clark). I thank Dr. Clinton Chase of Indiana University, who helped in my understanding of the statistical procedures used.

I also thank Evan Farber, head librarian at Earlham College; Larry Frye, library director at Wabash College; Grady Morein, formerly library director at the University of Evansville; and Mark Tucker, senior reference librarian at Purdue University. They arranged interviews, helped distribute and collect attitude scales, and provided other aid.

At Eckerd College, I thank Dr. Lloyd Chapin, dean of the faculty and vice-president for academic affairs. He encouraged my scholarship and allowed me a leave during part of the 1988/1989 academic year to complete this book. I thank my colleagues in the Eckerd College library for taking on many of my duties in my absence, particularly my fellow librarians—David Henderson and Jamie Hastreiter. I thank Ellen James, Lucie Dye, Harriet Turley, Catherine McCoy, and Cynthia Garrels for their contributions. I appreciate their enthusiastic responses to my frequent interlibrary loan requests.

Most important, I thank my wife, Carol, for her patience and encouragement. Unfortunately, we can never reclaim time once past. Finally, in recognition of their positive influence and many sacrifices, I thank my parents.

chapter one

INTRODUCTION

WHERE IS "THE HEART OF THE COLLEGE"?

One of the enigmas of higher education is the discrepancy between the often-stated and the actual role of the academic library in undergraduate education. On the one hand, many presidents, deans, and faculty members frequently refer to the library as "the heart of the college." All respectable colleges and universities have a library supported with a considerable investment of resources. On the other hand, substantial evidence suggests that the stated role of the library is largely an organizational fiction. Many studies reveal little or no use of a significant portion of library materials. Other studies show that many undergraduates neither use nor know how to use the library. Therefore, it is urgent that researchers examine the reasons for the discrepancy between the stated and actual role of the library in undergraduate education.

Among the members of the academic community who have a major influence on the development and use of the library are the faculty.[1] There is, however, an unclear understanding of the attitudes of faculty toward the undergraduate educational role of the library. We base the first part of this book on a study designed to identify and depict library educational attitudes of undergraduate classroom faculty. We developed an attitude scale to examine the elements or factors of library educational attitudes and to explore relationships between library educational attitudes and various demographic and academic variables of faculty members.

In the second part we relate the results of this study to the prevailing faculty attitudes and behaviors in American higher education. How did the present faculty culture develop and what are its prominent characteristics? How do faculty members' attitudes toward their teaching, research, and careers relate to their attitudes toward the role of the library in undergraduate education? How can librarians work within the framework of the

---

[1] Although we recognize that librarians also may be members of the faculty, for the sake of simplicity, faculty, as used throughout this book, refers to classroom faculty who teach undergraduates.

faculty culture to enhance the educational role of the library? Can the rhetoric about the library as the "heart of the college" become a reality?

DEVELOPMENT OF ACADEMIC LIBRARIES

The acquisition of books and related materials for American academic libraries during the past century has been nothing short of phenomenal. Even moderately sized college libraries today are larger than all but the largest university libraries of a century ago. In 1876 among principal academic libraries, only Harvard University's had more than 100,000 library volumes. Libraries at Bates, Bowdoin, DePauw, Haverford, Lafayette, and Oberlin held only between about 7,000 to 23,000 volumes each (Holley, 1976). In fact, in 1876 only Harvard exceeded the 1986 standards for college libraries of 100,000 volumes, including add-on stipulations (College Library Standards Committee, 1986). With the development of graduate education in the late 19th century and the post-World War II library boom, library holdings greatly expanded. By the mid-1980s the Harvard University libraries held more than 10 million volumes ("Holdings of Research Libraries in U.S., Canada," 1986). The libraries of Bates, Bowdoin, DePauw, Haverford, Lafayette, and Oberlin each increased to more than 400,000 volumes (*American Library Directory*, 1986), almost double the 212,000 volumes Harvard had in 1876. Even with the recent retrenchment in higher education, colleges and universities annually spend millions of dollars in the development and service of their libraries.

EDUCATIONAL CONTRIBUTION OF ACADEMIC LIBRARIES

Critics easily can argue that support of academic libraries is highly beneficial to higher education and to society. Nevertheless, considerable evidence suggests that libraries can contribute more to undergraduate education. Even before the post-World War II boom in academic libraries, Branscomb (1940), in his classic study *Teaching With Books*, raised this issue. He asked that given "the limited use which the majority of college students make of the library. . . . whether we need these large libraries, if present teaching methods continue?" (Branscomb, 1940, p. 8). A decade later, the eminent librarian Louis Round Wilson (Wilson, Lowell, & Reed, 1951) raised a similar issue when he wrote, "Although colleges spend a considerable portion of their educational budgets for library materials and services, the contribution that libraries make to furthering the educational program is less than it should be" (p. 13).

TABLE 1.1
Students Making Negligible Use of General Book Collection

Researcher	Year	Institution	Percent
Branscomb (1940)	Spring 1937 (2nd Half Spring Semester)	University A	66.9
Hardesty (1975)	Spring 1974 (2nd Half Spring Semester)	Kearney State	62.3
Hardesty (1980)	Spring 1976 (Spring Semester)	DePauw University	67.3

Note. Branscomb's definition of negligible use is the withdrawal of less than one book per month (1940, p. 29).

More recently, Gresham Riley, president of Colorado College, echoed the earlier thoughts of Branscomb and Wilson. In his address to several hundred academic librarians at the Third National Conference of the Association of College and Research Libraries, he stated emphatically and without contradiction from his audience, "Clearly, the library is not the heart of the college" (Riley, 1984, p. 12).

What evidence is there to support the conclusion that (in Wilson's words), "the contribution that the libraries make to furthering the educational program is less than it should be" (Wilson et al., 1951, p. 13)? Many studies dating from the 1930s to the present reveal that a large portion, even a majority, of undergraduates never borrow materials for use outside the library. Woods, in a 1965 masters paper, identified and analyzed 25 of these studies. During the 1970s we confirmed the continued validity of the earlier studies (see Table 1.1) (Hardesty, 1975, 1975/76, 1980).

Use studies also reveal that a large portion of library materials are seldom or never used. According to Broadus, library science professor at the University of North Carolina-Chapel Hill, "Use studies have pointed up the fact that in many libraries, especially large academic and research libraries, there are miles of books that are not borrowed for years and years" (Broadus, 1980, p. 317). The most important of these studies is the University of Pittsburgh study conducted during the 1970s. Kent and his colleagues found that about 40 percent of over 36,000 books acquired in 1969 had not circulated outside the library during their first six years (Kent et al., 1978).

Critics of the Pittsburgh study question its methodology (examination of recorded circulation). They contend this methodology more accurately reflected the pattern of undergraduate use than graduate and faculty use of the library (Borkowski & MacLeod, 1979a, 1979b, 1979c; Schad, 1979; Voigt, 1979). Even if we accept this criticism, studies at undergraduate

TABLE 1.2
General Collection Circulation

Number of Circulations	Institutions				
	Pittsburgh (5 Years)	DePauw (5 Years)	DePauw (3 Years)	Eckerd (3 Years)	Eckerd (4 Years)
0	44.7%	36.9%	44.3%	33.2%	26.3%
1–5	34.7	49.9	47.8	60.4	61.7
6–10	10.2	8.7	6.2	4.9	9.0
11+	10.4	4.5	1.7	1.7	2.9
Total Books	38,400	1,904	1,904	1,398	1,514

institutions support the conclusion of little or no use of a large portion of the collection.

Our studies at two liberal arts colleges, DePauw University and Eckerd College, show almost the same pattern of nonuse of library materials as at the University of Pittsburgh (see Table 1.2). At DePauw about 44 percent of the books acquired had not circulated at all after three years. Thirty-seven percent had not circulated after five years (Hardesty, 1981a). At Eckerd our first study showed about one-third of the books had not circulated after three years (Hardesty, 1988a).

Our second study at Eckerd showed that about one-fourth of the books did not circulate after four years (Hardesty, 1988b). In this study, over half the books selected by faculty members in some disciplines (French and mathematics) had not circulated after four years. Over one-third of the books selected by faculty members in such library-oriented disciplines as literature and religion had not circulated after four years.

A study among the Associated Colleges of the Midwest (ACM) used random and nonrandom stack and circulation samples to study book use. This study found that 40 percent of the test libraries' collections satisfied 80 percent of users' measurable circulation needs (Trochim, 1981). At the University of Pittsburgh about 20 percent of the collection accounted for 80 percent of the circulation. At DePauw University and Eckerd College about 30 percent and about 34 percent, respectively, accounted for 80 percent of the circulation. Even the ACM study found areas of no use within the collections of these small academic libraries (A. Miller, Jr., personal communication, November 18, 1985).

These results, as Lancaster (1988) reported, "shocked many people and many were inclined to disbelieve" (p. 37). Nevertheless, these results should not surprise librarians. Examination of the reserve collection provides further support for the conclusion that a large portion of the general collection receives little or no use. We found at DePauw that over 40 percent of the reserve collection books did not circulate during a semester-long study (Hardesty, 1981b). Therefore, even books selected by faculty members for extensive student use through the reserve collection often remain unused. Unlike what critics frequently claim for general collection books, students cannot read and reshelve reserve books without a record of use.

Since, however, recorded circulation is an imprecise measure, we must interpret with care use studies based on this methodology. Broadus pointed out that a student may check out a book for 10 minutes or 20 hours. During that time one person or several people may read the book (Broadus, 1980). Hamburg, Clelland, Bommer, Ramist, and Whitfield (1974) provide a rationale for counting each circulation as equal. They assumed that a circulation represents an exposure to a document. This, in turn, enhances an individual's self-development and, thus, it is a benefit to society. The amount of societal benefit does not vary greatly from one document exposure to another.

Unrecorded or in-house use is even more difficult to measure. Nevertheless, several researchers have addressed this issue. They found a strong relationship between recorded circulation and in-house use of books (Bommer, 1971; Domas, 1978; Fussler & Simon, 1969; Galvin & Kent, 1977; Hardesty, 1988a; Hindle & Buckland, 1978; McGrath, 1971; Sheridan, 1979). In fact, Bommer found an almost linear relationship between recorded circulation and in-house use of books with almost one in-house use for each recorded circulation. Harris (1977) and Stockard, Griffin, and Coblyn (1978) found a less defined relationship. Stockard et al. concluded, "factors unique to each library, such as subject focus, characteristics of clientele, holdings, access, seating capacity, and loan policies influence in-house use" (p. 141). Nevertheless, despite the imprecision of use studies, the evidence supports the conclusion of little or no use of the academic library.

THE FACULTY'S ROLE

The library literature from the 1930s to the present belies the myth of an earlier "golden age" of library involvement in undergraduate education. Never have large numbers of self-motivated, highly capable undergraduates converged on the library. Obviously, many groups share responsibility for the status of the library in undergraduate education: students, librarians, administrators, and faculty. Most librarians consider the faculty's role dominant—and negative!

After examining several studies from the 1930s, Branscomb (1940) as early as 1940, "Books bought by the library lie unused on the shelves because instructors in large numbers are not depending upon these volumes to supply any essential element in the educational process for which they are responsible" (p. 79). Nearly 20 years later, Knapp (1958) reached a similar conclusion:

> Neither subject field, nor teaching method, nor kind of assignment, nor quality of students in a class is of crucial importance in determining whether or not a given course will be dependent upon the library. The only decisive factor seemed to be—and this is a subjective judgment—the instructor's attitude. Where the instructor expected and planned for student use, it occurred. Where he did not, it did not occur. (p. 829)

In the early 1960s the eminent librarian Guy Lyle (1963) commented:

> The faculty have the primary responsibility for structuring the academic courses for independent study. Present teaching practices would appear to provide little incentive for students to do substantial and rewarding reading. If professors are wedded to the idea of using textbooks and reserve readings, there is little the librarian can do about making changes. (p. 56)

In the early 1970s Wilkinson (1971) still could refer to libraries as largely successful only as study halls. Young (1974), after an extensive literature review, could unequivocally assert, "The dominant role of the instructor in influencing library use is beyond question" (p. 5). Many other librarians by the 1970s shared this view, such as Kirk (1974), Collins (1978), Holland (1978), and Merrill (1979).

From the 1960s to the early 1980s the National Endowment for the Humanities and the Council on Library Resources funded programs to enhance the library's educational role. About three million dollars went to more than 50 academic libraries. In 1980 Gwinn reviewed these programs. Her review closed an important period in library use history. She found librarians frequently mentioned difficulties with faculty members among the largest problems in setting up programs. The difficulties included: (a) poor cooperation from faculty, (b) faculty and administrative turnover, and (c) lack of adequate planning with faculty input. Despite problems with library staff turnover and lack of administrative enthusiasm, she concluded, "building faculty relations—getting out of the library and into campus affairs—is still the key to building support for the library's instructional role and other services" (p. 10). Librarians must reach out to the faculty because of the faculty dominance.

Other librarians have called for librarians to reach out to the faculty. Lyle (1974), in his standard work on academic library administration, *The Administration of the College Library*, and Biggs (1981), in her review of relations between librarians and faculty, called for librarians to take the initiative in communicating and cooperating with the faculty. In fact, Biggs placed the burden squarely on librarians. She concluded that librarians have created a "nearly insuperable barrier" (p. 196) by their reluctance to confront the faculty. Before librarians can achieve success in their initiatives, however, they must understand the faculty.

FACULTY'S LIBRARY-RELATED ATTITUDES

What do we know about the faculty's library-related attitudes? Unfortunately, faculty comments about the library are usually anecdotal, often speculative, and occasionally simplistic. For example, Blackburn (1968), a respected professor of higher education, analyzed college libraries enough to conclude, "Very simply put, faculty members want to own (possess) books even more than they want students to love books" (p. 172). Weintraub (1980), a graduate dean of humanities, wrote in his analysis of scholars and libraries:

> Their [humanistic scholars'] appetite for books is insatiable. They simply feel better by being surrounded by books—of which they can only read a fraction; one of their early patron saints, Francesco Petrarca, started this by holding forth eloquently about his Greek copy of Homer—which he could not read. (p. 25)

All this makes for interesting (and inflammatory) reading. It, however, does little to further understanding of faculty attitudes toward the library's role in undergraduate education.

For the librarians' perspective, we can start with Harvie Branscomb. From his early analyses of several studies, Branscomb found it "painfully apparent" that faculty "have not learned how to make very effective use of the library in their teaching" (1940, p. 8). He also found few faculty members interested in learning how to make effective use of the library. He concluded that student accomplishments through the textbook and classroom discussions satisfy most faculty members.

Through her experiences at Knox College in the 1950s and in the Monteith College Project during the 1960s, Knapp probed the faculty view of the library. She found that many faculty members relied on reserve books and highly selected readings. Faculty members believed this to be the only way for students to identify important works and to understand the discipline's organization, terminology, concepts, and methods (Knapp, 1966b). Many faculty members believed that only in small classes could they give the individual attention to students needed to guide and stimulate library use. Knapp determined that many faculty members regarded only the advanced students to have the capability for, and the interest in, extensive library use. For these faculty members, only potential graduate students needed a high level of library competence (Knapp, 1958).

Knapp found that bibliographic instruction tools developed by librarians emphasized subject and form of publication. Faculty emphasized discipline, concept, and method (Knapp, 1966a). She concluded:

> Most college faculty members see library instruction as dealing with bits of information, undeniably useful, but fragmented, not related to any single, coherent, framework, not calling for problem-solving behavior, for critical thinking, for imagination. (Knapp, 1966b, p. 89)

In her overall analysis, Knapp (1965) suggested, "sophisticated understanding of the library and increasing competence in its use as a goal of general education is not accepted, perhaps not understood by most of the faculty" (p. 262).

Both Lindgren and Knapp found that many faculty members considered the library easy to use. These faculty members assumed an hour's time is enough for anything worth teaching about the library (Lindgren, 1978). Similarly, Knapp (1959) reported some faculty who assumed, "desirable library habits, interests, knowledge, and skills, are 'picked up' by all or almost all students as needed when the occasion for them arises" (pp. 94–95).

Two influential librarians, Louis Round Wilson (Wilson et al., 1951) and Evan Farber (1974a) have provided a rationale for the library-related attitudes of faculty. They hypothesized about relationships between the faculty's background and their library-related attitudes. Farber and Lyle both regarded faculty ill-prepared to select library materials for use in teaching programs and to stimulate student library use. Farber termed his hypothesis the "university-library syndrome." He explained:

> The faculty members' academic background and training work against an understanding of the proper role of the college library. He has been trained as a scholar-researcher and is not really interested in *how* his students use the library; he, after all, learned to use it in his discipline and he assumes students can also. . . . Rarely does it occur to him that learning how to use the library intelligently and independently is not only a desirable part of the educational process but will also permit students to do better work for him. (1974a, pp. 16–17)

Faculty members, according to Farber, are "*not* predisposed *as scholars* emphasis his to recognize and to acknowledge a legitimate educational role for the library and for librarians" (1974a, p. 12).

In one of the few empirical studies in this area, Cameron and Messinger (1975) found that librarians placed more emphasis than did faculty members on the general education potential of the academic library. This diversity affects faculty-librarian relations, according to Biggs (1981), because of a tendency among faculty to view the library from a narrow individual or departmental perspective. Riley (1984), a college president, emphasized the importance of local conditions in shaping faculty's attitudes. He stressed the importance of key administrators' attitudes in influencing faculty's attitudes toward the library. We cannot fully answer here whether faculty members develop their attitudes from graduate training or later from experiences as a faculty member but we will discuss this issue later.

Another highly influential academic librarian, Guy Lyle, emphasized the risks for the faculty in involving students in use of the library. He concluded that the faculty member "who embarks on a program of engaging students actively in learning for themselves through independent library use is a bit of a gambler and takes chances" (1974, p. 108). The faculty member who, according to Lyle, thinks only of his own course and "who confines himself to the troika of lecture, textbook, and assigned readings—all of his own choosing—has tradition and experience to assure his success" (1974, p. 108).

Others have suggested that faculty members do not look to the library as a source of information. Dougherty and Blomquist (1974) found that many faculty members use personal collections and departmental reading rooms. Faculty members often considered these sources more important in their teaching and research than the academic library. Recently the American Council of Learned Societies (ACLS) surveyed humanities and social science scholars. These scholars ranked the library a distant third for keeping up in their fields. Both personal libraries and recently bought materials ranked ahead of libraries (Morton & Price, 1986). Merrill (1979) found that faculty members reported as irregular library users showed a preference for their personal collections as their primary source of research materials. We do not know whether the faculty are unfamiliar with the library resources or simply find it inconvenient to use the library. Investigations by Hernon (1979) on the use of government publications by social scientists support both conclusions.

Marchant (1969), a library science professor, and Blackburn (1968) offer the most critical explanation for faculty attitudes toward the library. According to Marchant (1969), faculty members consider the library a threat to their position or goals. Similarly, Blackburn (1968) concluded books compete with faculty members as a source of information. Students may find in books views contrary to those of the faculty member. We believe both overstated the negative view.

CONCLUSIONS

Despite the library's enormous growth it has not evolved into "the heart of the college." The classroom still has a lock on that title, and may always. The keepers of the classroom also determine the library's fortune. We, however, have little insight into their vision. What do they want from us? Why do some call for more periodicals and books? Yet, we never see their students in the library. In fact, we may not even see them in the library. Why do others, a small minority by all accounts, carefully integrate student use of the library into their classes? How do they differ from their colleagues?

Attitudes are the key. Librarians, as stewards of the library, have a responsibility to inquire into the faculty's library-related attitudes. Librarians must develop an understanding of the needs and aspirations of the faculty. Through a better understanding of faculty's library attitudes, librarians can enhance the library's role in undergraduate education.

chapter two

ATTITUDE AND ITS MEASUREMENT

THE CONCEPT OF ATTITUDE

To appreciate the significance of library-related attitudes, we must understand the essence of the psychological construct *attitude*. Pioneer social psychologist Gordon Allport (1968) called it "the primary building stone in the edifice of social psychology" (p. 63). "Attitude," commented Lemon (1973), "is one of the most ubiquitous of all the terms used in the social sciences" (p. 1). What is the meaning of this term pervasive even in our everyday language? How did attitude theory develop? How do attitudes and behaviors relate? How do we measure attitudes?

In 1935, after he examined some 16 earlier definitions, Allport offered what has become the most widely used and accepted definition. He defined attitude as "a mental and neural state of readiness, organized through experience, exerting a directive or dynamic influence upon the individual's response to all objects and situations with which it is related" (1935, p. 35). Others have added definitions to the literature (Bany & Johnson, 1975; McGuire 1969). Nevertheless, two aspects of Allport's definition remain particularly important. First, individuals *learn* attitudes, and, second, attitudes *relate to behavior*.

In 1948, Krech and Crutchfield offered the second important contribution to the definition of attitude through emphasis on its *persistent* characteristics. In the late 1960s, Shaw and Wright (1967) extracted the common features of earlier definitions. They stressed the *drive-producing response* that gives rise to overt behavior related to attitude. Later, Osgood, Suci, and Tannebaum (1970) distinguished attitude from other states of readiness. Attitudes, they wrote, involved *evaluative responses*. Individuals can ascribe their responses to a bipolar continuum with tendencies of approach or avoidance and a neutral or zero point. Osgood's et al. contribution relates particularly to measurement of attitude.

Other researchers, such as Rokeach (1968), have elaborated on its definition. Nevertheless, many researchers consider definitions provided after Allport's as little more than variations of his ideas. A review of psychology textbooks, such as those by Kerlinger (1973) and Anastasi (1982), supports this position.

Variations, however, do exist among definitions of attitude, and social psychologists argue the distinctions. Nevertheless, Oppenheim (1966), in his review of attitude, cautioned readers about dwelling too much on the logic of attitudes. He wrote:

> Attitudes are only very rarely the product of a balanced conclusion after a careful assembly of evidence; as a rule, attitudes are acquired or modified by absorbing, or reacting to, the attitudes of other people. We like to maintain the fiction of rationality and impartiality in reaching our conclusions, but, in fact, attitudinal predispositions play a very considerable part. One must remember always that attitudes are highly emotional, both in the sense of irrational or illogical and in the sense of arousing powerful needs and ego defenses . . . this is where research can help—by showing the underlying attitude links, with their strong emotional connections. (pp. 111–112)

The complexities of attitudes are no more clear than when we explore their relationships with behaviors.

THE ATTITUDE AND BEHAVIOR LINK

Newcomb (1966) noted that sociologists and psychologists often defined attitude through the likelihood of a specific behavior occurring in a specific situation. Such definitions, he remarked, "serve to remind us that the ultimate reference of attitude is behavior" (p. 23). In fact, we cannot see attitudes directly but must infer them from behavior. Attitude researchers assume that behavioral expressions of attitude allow us to understand and to predict other behaviors (Newcomb, 1966). Indeed, to show attitude research as useful to decision makers, we must identify the extent to which attitudes affects behaviors. Decision makers express little interest in attitudes. Instead, they focus on behaviors (Liska, 1974).

The relationship between attitude and behavior has long been a subject of considerable controversy. Critics of any consistent relationship between the two frequently cite LaPiere's (1934) classic early study. LaPiere found a clear discrepancy between a Chinese couple's treatment by some 250 hotels, restaurants, and similar establishments and the stated policies of these establishments. Eagley and Himmelfarb (1978) concluded that by the late 1960s many widely read papers emphasized that attitudes poorly predicted behavior. Many social scientists regarded the hypothesis nearly useless.

More recently, however, Gross and Niman (1985) analyzed explanations of the seeming lack of consistency between attitude and behavior. They found any lack of consistency usually explained by one or more personal, situational, and methodological factors. Ajzen and Fishbein (1977), in an influential literature review, criticized earlier research. They considered many measures of attitude and behavior selected on a theoretically arbitrary basis. Ajzen and Fishbein determined that an individual's attitude towards an object influences the overall pattern of his or her responses to the object. Yet, they concluded, it need not predict any given action.

Ragan and Fazio (1977), Liska (1974), and Kelman (1974) all supported a strong relationship between attitudes and behaviors. In his analysis, Kelman emphasized the importance of both social constraints and the interaction between attitudes and behaviors. He found when researchers considered social constraints in studies showing weak relationships between attitude and behavior, "the findings fall neatly into place" (p. 313).

Gross and Niman (1985) pointed out that the distinction between attitude and behavior can be misleading. Individuals exhibit behavior through both written and verbal attitude responses. In addition, individual's overt behavior often lack consistency (Lemon, 1973). In many circumstances, verbal behavior more accurately displays attitude than do observations of nonverbal behavior (Edwards, 1957). In their review of the literature, Cialdini, Petty, and Cacioppo (1981) concluded, "The prevailing view of the ability of attitudes to predict and cause behavior has rarely been more positive" (p. 358). According to these authors, the question now is not *if* attitudes predict behaviors, but *when* attitudes predict behavior.

THE MEASUREMENT OF ATTITUDES

Even if attitudes relate to behavior, how can we adequately measure attitudes—obviously an important question since this book focuses on attitude measurement? Measurement, as defined by psychologist Nunnally (1978), is a set of "rules for assigning numbers to objects in such a way as to represent quantities of attributes" (p. 1). How do we assign the numbers? At first glance we might first select overt behavior.

Cook and Selltiz (1964), however, pointed out that overt responses may vary from private responses, which limits use of overt behavior. Even with the absence of efforts to distort responses, factors other than attitude may influence behavior. They found observations of overt behavior at least as sensitive as self-report methods to extraneous factors. In addition, for replication purposes, they concluded, "Situations capable of eliciting behavior toward an attitudinal object are more difficult to devise and to standardize, and more time consuming and costly to manage, than self-report measures" (p. 44). For these reasons, the self-report method clearly has become the dominant approach to attitude measurement (Summers, 1970).

Researchers have developed many techniques for attitude measurement. The Thurstone and Likert methods, however, remain the two most widely used. Thurstone and Chave (1929) developed the equal-interval method first in the late 1920s. Likert (1932) soon followed in the early 1930s with his summative method. Most behavioral research textbooks (Anastasi, 1982; Kerlinger, 1973; Nunnally, 1978) thoroughly describe these methods. Several authors have compared the two techniques.

Seiler and Hough (1970) concluded that the Likert method consistently produces more reliable results for any given number of items. Only 20 to 25 items often produce high reliabilities (.90 or more) (refer to Appendix A for a discussion of reliability). Edwards and Kenny (1946) suggested in an early comparison that the Likert method is less time consuming and laborious. Edwards (1957) later concluded that they appeared fairly equal in these areas. Each method has supporters, but attitude researchers today prefer the Likert method. Kerlinger (1973) termed it the "most useful method in behavioral research" (p. 499). Lemon (1973) concluded it is "justifiably the most popular method of attitude scale construction in use today" (p. 182).

SUMMARY

Throughout the past half-century social psychologists have developed a good understanding of attitudes. They have linked attitudes to behaviors. Intervening factors, however, often obscure the link. Nevertheless, when carefully developed, self-report measurement techniques provide satisfactory and important avenues for investigating attitudes. Careful application of established techniques allowed us to study faculty members' attitudes toward the role of the library in undergraduate education.

chapter three

RESEARCH METHODOLOGY

PURPOSE OF THE STUDY

We sought to achieve three main goals in the study. First, and most important, we sought to develop an attitude scale which would accurately describe the library-related educational attitudes of undergraduate faculty members. This goal's achievement should aid librarians and others in understanding faculty's attitudes toward the library's role in undergraduate education. In addition, we hoped that others would use the attitude scale to replicate the study at other institutions. Through replication we can probe the wider application of the findings of this study.

Second, and closely related to the first goal, we sought to reveal various elements or factors within library educational attitudes. We used exploratory factor analysis to determine these elements. As the reader will see, this procedure allowed us in-depth examination of the complexities of library-related attitudes.

Third, we used the attitude scale developed to examine the relationships between library educational attitudes and various characteristics of the faculty. We should expect faculty members, as complex individuals, to hold varying attitudes toward the library. In scrutinizing various academic and demographic variables of faculty members, we gained an insight into the development of their particular library-related attitudes.

METHODOLOGY

To achieve the goals, we used qualitative and quantitative techniques designed to provide both depth and breadth to the results. The techniques involved six major steps. First, we selected or developed suitable definitions of terms used. Second, we located and selected applicable criteria for attitude-scale construction. Third, we applied the criteria and constructed attitude-scale items. To develop statements representative of faculty library-related attitudes, we reviewed the literature, used personal experiences, and conducted interviews of appropriate individuals. Fourth, we refined the attitude scale items through use of judges and a pilot test of the attitude scale. Fifth, we field tested the attitude scale. As our last step, we organized, analyzed, and interpreted the results of the field test data.

Definitions of Terms

The attitudes measured need a clear definition for the development of a useful attitude scale. Since the reader may be unfamiliar with attitude research, we have provided definitions of both *attitude* and *library educational attitudes*. We reviewed several definitions of the psychological construct *attitude* proposed in the literature and noted their contributions. Despite the variations, the basic elements in attitude definitions remain similar. To support our use of the definition of attitudes, we looked to Rokeach (1968), source of the most extensive recent review of attitude definitions. He concluded researchers could interchange the various attitude definitions for attitude measurement purposes. In particular, we borrowed heavily from the operationalized definition conceived by Sherif and Sherif (1969, p. 33).

> *Attitude*: An individual's set of categories for rating with varying degrees of positive and negative effect a learned readiness to act in a predisposed manner towards certain objects, people, ideas, and other referents.

This definition supports two crucial assumptions of this study. First, a relationship exists between attitudes and behaviors. Second, attitudes range between negative and positive degrees, measurable by an attitude scale.

Since we dealt with a subset of attitudes concerned with the library's role in undergraduate education, we needed to define that subset. Therefore, we developed a definition based on Morstain and Smart's (1976, p. 1200) definition of general educational attitudes.

> *Library Educational Attitudes*: Attitudes toward the role of the library in achieving the goals and purposes of undergraduate education, and toward methods of using the library in achieving these goals and purposes.

Attitude-Scale Construction

In seeking to explore the dimensions of library educational attitudes, we hypothesized that faculty members, in fact, would have attitudes toward several library-related factors. We expected they would have specific views of the abilities and motivations of undergraduates toward the academic library. We envisioned they would have thoughts about the role of librarians in undergraduate education. We believed that faculty members had views about their responsibilities and the educational role of the library. On less certain ground, we decided to explore the faculty members' attitudes toward administrators' role in developing and promoting the library in undergraduate education. Finally, we speculated faculty members might have definite ideas and expectations about the physical characteristics of the library. In this grouping, we included questions on study areas, building aesthetics, hours open, and related matters.

An attitude scale provides a convenient way of determining the dimensions of the attitudes of large numbers of individuals. Thus, it offers breadth to a study. This breadth, however, results in a shallow study unless the researcher carefully constructed the scale. Together, the attitude scale items or statements must represent the scope of the attitude studied.

To bring depth to the study, we reviewed the literature of both academic librarianship and higher education for representative attitude statements. In addition, we relied on our own knowledge for some statements. Personal interviews, however, provided most of the attitude statements. As pointed out by Katz and Kahn (1966), personal interviews aid the exploration of attitudes in a depth not readily possible through surveys and questionnaires. Therefore, we decided to make extensive use of interviews, and followed Oppenheim's (1966) recommendation as to the number necessary to gather information for attitude scale development.

We included four major types of institutions. The University of Evansville represented small comprehensive universities. Purdue University and Indiana University represented major research universities. Indiana State University and Ball State University represented medium-sized state universities. Earlham College and Wabash College represented private liberal arts colleges. We hypothesized that these seven institutions would have faculty members and librarians that represented a wide range of library educational attitudes.

We used a semistructured interview guide. This type of guide offers the opportunity to gain in-depth information from a relatively small sample of individuals in a limited amount of time (Stewart & Cash, 1974). We pilot tested the guide with three faculty members at the University of Evansville. We then interviewed at least two faculty members in each of the three general disciplinary areas (sciences, social sciences, and humanities) at the other institutions. At each institution, we asked a librarian to arrange interviews with faculty members. We relied on the librarian's judgment to select the faculty members. We requested that half the faculty members should represent positive attitudes and half should represent negative attitudes toward the library. In this manner we hoped to gather both positive and negative attitude statements. We conducted all interviews individually with the faculty members. Each interview lasted 45 to 90 minutes. We used handwritten notes to record interviews, as recommended by Guba and Lincoln (1981). At the seven colleges and universities, we interviewed 40 faculty members and seven librarians.

From our notes we prepared 130 attitude statements. Deletion of redundant and unclear statements reduced the total attitude statements to 90. Six academic librarians and six faculty members, selected for their interest in undergraduate education, served as judges. They examined these statements against a specified set of criteria and suggested wording changes. They also responded to the attitude statements and classified the attitude statements for validation purposes.

Based on comments and responses of the 12 judges, we judged 20 attitude statements not useful. We then slightly changed the remaining statements. This resulted in 70 attitude statements for a second set of judges. Selected on the same basis as the earlier judges, these six judges also used the same criteria to rate the statements. Based on the recommendations of these judges, we dropped 10 more attitude statements.

The attitude scale now consisted of 60 items in a Likert-type format. We used seven steps ranging from *strongly agree* to *strongly disagree* with a neutral point. Next, we tested the attitude scale with the 40 faculty members and seven librarians originally interviewed. All 47 individuals responded, and 45 of the responses proved useful for analysis. From an analysis of the results, we developed the final attitude scale.

Field Test of the Attitude Scale

The final attitude scale consisted of 15 positive and 15 negative statements with a Likert-type format. We field tested it at four colleges and universities in the state of Indiana: Earlham College, University of Evansville, Purdue University, and Wabash College. We selected these institution because we expected diversity among the faculty on their library educational attitudes. Such difference are important in showing attitude scale validity (see Appendix A).

For example, Earlham College is a small liberal arts college well known for extensive involvement of the academic library in undergraduate education. Purdue University is a major research university. We included only the undergraduate biology faculty members at Purdue University in the field test. Supported by the judges, we hypothesized that undergraduate science faculty members at a research university would be less positive towards an active role of the library in undergraduate education than would faculty members at the other institutions. We hypothesized that the faculty members at Wabash College and the University of Evansville would hold attitudes about the library somewhere between those held by the faculty members surveyed at Purdue University and Earlham College.

We intended the attitude scale only for use among undergraduate faculty members in the traditional liberal arts. Therefore, the field test included only those individuals who met this criteria at each institution. We excluded graduate faculty members and faculty members teaching preprofessional areas, such as engineering, social work, and business.

LIMITATIONS

The research methodology described, of course, has certain limitations. We are not free from personal bias about the library's role in undergraduate education. In fact, we support a very active role for the library. We did try to guard against this bias from interfering with the study. Nevertheless, it may have influenced the interview questions asked and the statements selected for the attitude scale. In a sense, we have taken only a one-time glimpse of a few faculty members' library-related attitudes.

Having pointed out some of the limitations of this study's methodology, we must note its strengths. The faculty members spoke freely and at some length about their views and allowed us to probe deeply. A surprisingly large proportion of them completed and returned the attitude scale. Neither in the interviews nor on the attitude scale did they show that any of our biases influenced them. In addition, as shown in this chapter, we applied most rigorously the methodology used. The results, discussed in the following chapter, show that we have gained useful information that stands up under scrutiny.

chapter four

THE FACULTY AND THEIR LIBRARY ATTITUDES*

INTRODUCTION

In this chapter we provide descriptive information on the general characteristics of the responding faculty members. We then relate these characteristics to their library attitudes. Librarians long have speculated about the attitudes of faculty members. Some librarians presume younger faculty members are the most receptive to involving undergraduates in the library. Others believe humanities faculty members are the most interested in directing students to the library. Others think only at small liberal arts colleges do faculty members indeed involve the library.

GENERAL CHARACTERISTICS OF THE RESPONDING FACULTY MEMBERS

We asked 292 faculty members to complete the 30-item *Library Educational Attitude Scale* (LEAS). Two hundred thirty-four faculty members returned the completed scales for an overall response rate of 80.1 percent. As shown by Table 4.1, the response rate varied from institution to institution. We, however, did not find a significantly different response rate among the institutions. We assumed the high response rate provided an accurate reflection of the faculty members' attitudes at each institution.

We classified the respondents into four broad disciplinary groups: humanities, social sciences, sciences, and fine arts (see Table 4.2). Junior ranks (instructor or assistant professor) accounted for 37 percent of the

---

* Portions of this chapter were previously published as Hardesty, L. (1984). The Influence of Selected Variables on Attitudes of Classroom Instructors Toward the Undergraduate Educational Role of the Academic Library. In Suzanne C. Dodson and Gary L. Menges (Eds.), *Academic Libraries: Myths and Realities; Proceedings of the Third National Conference of the Association of College and Research Libraries* (pp. 365–372). Chicago: Association of College and Research Libraries.

TABLE 4.1
Distribution of Respondents by Institution

	Earlham	Evansville	Purdue	Wabash	Total
Respondents	68 (86%)	80 (75%)	29 (74%)	57 (84%)	234 (80.1%)
Nonrepondents	11 (14%)	26 (25%)	10 (26%)	11 (16%)	58 (19.9%)
Totals	79	106	39	68	292

Note. Chi Square = 5.65; Chi Square at .01 with 3 degrees of freedom is 11.345; cannot reject the null hypothesis of no significant differences among the rate of return among the four institutions.

TABLE 4.2
Distribution of Respondents by Discipline

	Earlham	Evansville	Purdue	Wabash	Total
Fine Art	7	17	0	6	30 (12.8%)
Humanities	29	23	0	25	77 (33%)
Sciences	18	16	29	17	80 (34.2%)
Social Sciences	14	24	0	8	46 (19.6%)
No Indication	0	0	0	1	1 (00.4%)
Totals	69	80	29	57	234

TABLE 4.3
Distribution of Respondents by Rank

	Earlham	Evansville	Purdue	Wabash	Total
Instructor	0	3	1	2	6 (3.0%)
Asst. Prof.	25	29	8	18	80 (34.2%)
Assoc. Prof.	16	19	10	16	61 (26.0%)
Professor	27	29	10	20	86 (36.7%)
No Indication	0	0	0	1	1 (00.4%)
Totals	68	80	29	57	234

respondents. Senior ranks (associate or full professor) accounted for 63 percent (see Table 4.3). About 64 percent reported they had tenure (see Table 4.4). Eighty percent of the respondents reported the doctorate as their highest degree.

The responding faculty members represented considerable teaching experience. About one-third had taught for at least 16 years, and another 40 percent had taught between 6 and 15 years (see Table 4.5). We found about one-third of the faculty members relatively recent at their institution. About one-fourth had taught 16 years or longer at their present institution (see Table 4.6). Twenty percent reported ages of 51 years or older, and

TABLE 4.4
Distribution of Respondents by Tenure

	Earlham	Evansville	Purdue	Wabash	Total
Untenured	28	19	8	17	72 (30.7%)
Tenured	39	58	21	33	151 (64.5%)
No Indication	1	3	0	7	11 (4.7%)
Totals	68	80	29	57	234

TABLE 4.5
Distribution of Respondents by Total Years Taught

Number of Years	Earlham	Evansville	Purdue	Wabash	Total
0–5	10	12	7	8	37 (15.8%)
6–15	31	34	11	17	93 (39.7%)
16–25	15	21	6	15	57 (24.3%)
25+	7	7	3	5	22 (9.4%)
Not Indicated	5	6	2	12	25 (10.7%)
Totals	68	80	29	57	234

TABLE 4.6
Distribution of Respondents by Total Years Taught at Present Institution

Number of Years	Earlham	Evansville	Purdue	Wabash	Total
0–5	23	23	9	18	73 (31.2%)
6–15	26	32	10	9	77 (32.9%)
16–25	11	18	6	17	52 (22.2%)
25+	5	1	2	2	10 (4.2%)
Not Indicated	3	6	2	11	22 (9.4%)
Totals	68	80	29	57	234

another 50 percent reported their ages as between 36 and 50. Males made up about 85 percent of the respondents.

Some of the faculty members interviewed in the development of the attitude statements and surveyed in the pilot test also participated in the field test. We included seven faculty members from Earlham, three from Evansville, two from Purdue, and five (one did not respond) from Wabash. These 17 faculty members represented about 7 percent of all respondents. These participants could have become sensitized to the issues or in some

TABLE 4.7
Distribution of Respondents by Region of Institution Awarding Highest Degree

Region	Earlham	Evansville	Purdue	Wabash	Total
Midwest	25	58	12	33	128 (54.7%)
Northeast	26	12	10	16	64 (27.4%)
South	5	6	1	5	17 (7.3%)
West	7	4	3	2	16 (6.8%)
Non-U.S.	5	0	1	0	6 (2.6%)
Not Indicated	0	0	2	1	3 (1.3%)
Totals	68	80	29	57	234

other way skewed the results. We, however, did not find any differences between their responses and the responses of the other faculty.[1]

We did not compare these characteristics of the respondents with those of faculty of higher education in general to support claims of external validity. Nevertheless, as shown in later discussions, we believe such a comparison unnecessary. We did look at the source of the highest degree of the responding faculty members. As shown in Table 4.7, most of the faculty had received their highest degrees from institutions in the Midwest. We doubt this skewed the results of this study.

EXAMINING THE RELATIONSHIPS

Age, Rank, Tenure, and Teaching

The variables of age, rank, tenure, and teaching experience related highly to each other (see Table 4.8). In academia, with age obviously also comes experience, rank, and tenure, but not necessarily more positive library attitudes. Statistically, we could not find any significant relationships between library attitudes and these variables. For example, we placed faculty members into three age groups (26 to 35, 36 to 50, and 51 years and over). Among these groups, we found no significant differences in library attitudes. Neither youth nor age alone influenced the library attitudes of these faculty members (see Table 4.9).

Rank also made no difference as the library attitudes of faculty members (see Table 4.10). At first examination we thought tenure made a difference. Once, however, we accounted for the influence of institution, we

---

[1] A *t*-test did not result in the rejection of the null hypothesis of no significant difference between the average scale scores (average score of interviewed faculty [17] = 144.4, standard deviation = 19.0; average score of other faculty [217] = 139.9, standard deviation = 17.3; degrees of freedom = 232, probability = .01).

TABLE 4.8
Correlation Matrix Among Selected Variables

Variable	Age	Rank	Tenure[a]	Total Teaching
Rank	.70			
Tenure[a]	.58	.68		
Total Teaching	.88	.72	.59	
Teaching at Institution	.81	.72	.65	.88

Note. All correlations significant at .01 level.
[a]Recoded for positive correlation.

TABLE 4.9
ANOVA Summary Table of Average Scores by Age

Source	Degrees of Freedom	Sum of Squares	Mean Squares	F Ratio	F Prob.
Between Groups	2	78.41	39.21	.13	.88
Among Groups	222	69,538.97	313.24		
Total	224	69,617.38			

TABLE 4.10
ANOVA Summary Table of Average Scores By Rank

Source	Degrees of Freedom	Sum of Squares	Mean Squares	F Ratio	F Prob.
Between Groups	2	502.5	251.3	.825	.44
Among Groups	230	70,019.8	304.4		
Total	232	70,522.3			

Note. Instructor and assistant professor ranks combined.

could not distinguish between the attitudes of tenured and untenured faculty members (see Table 4.11).

We did find some differences in library attitudes according to the number of years faculty members had taught at their present institution (see Table 4.12). We found at Evansville that more experienced faculty members had more negative library attitudes. At Purdue, we found just the opposite. Perhaps faculty members may change library attitudes over time. Also possible, faculty members hired at one time may have different attitudes than those hired at another time. Finally, as suggested during the interviews at Earlham College, an institution may employ faculty members who hold attitudes the institution desires. Later experiences at the institu-

TABLE 4.11
ANOVA Summary Table of Average Scores by Tenure within Institution

Source	Degrees of Freedom	Sum of Squares	Mean Squares	F Ratio	F Prob.
Between Groups	4	11,848.10	2,962.02	11.50	.00
Institution	3	11,761.38	3,920.46	15.36	.00
Tenure	1	21.85	21.85	.09	.77
Interaction	3	1,983.21	661.07	2.59	.054
Residual	215	54,869.51	255.21		
Total	222	68,700.81	309.46		

TABLE 4.12
Correlations Between Attitude Score and Years Taught at Present Institution

Institution	Correlation	Significance	Number
Earlham	.05	.68	65
Evansville	−.30*	.01	74
Purdue	.41**	.035	27
Wabash	.09	.57	46
Total	−.02	.77	212

*Significant at .01.
**Significant at .05.

tion may only reinforce the attitudes. Based on only the information in Table 4.12, we cannot generalize about the influence of employment practices or local conditions.

Influence of the Doctorate

Both Farber (1974a) and Wilson et al. (1951) emphasized the influence of faculty members' graduate training. Graduate study and research usually consists of an intense period of socialization. We surmised that faculty members with doctorates might hold different library attitudes than those with only masters degrees. When, however, we tested our hypothesis we could not find any differences between attitudes of the two groups (two-tailed probability: .936; degrees of freedom: 228).

Source of Highest Degree

Previous experiences may influence faculty members' library attitudes. Since most of the faculty members had received their highest degree from midwestern institutions, we determined whether or not this had skewed

TABLE 4.13
ANOVA Summary Table by Attitudes and Region of Institution Awarding Highest Degree

Source	Degrees of Freedom	Sum of Squares	Mean Squares	F Ratio	F Prob.
Between Groups	4	360.12	90.03	.29	.88
Among Groups	226	69,716.39	308.48		
Total	230	70,076.51			

our results. Earlham faculty members, for example, had a large representation from northeastern institutions. Midwestern institutions served as a larger source of Evansville's faculty than for any other institutions. We, however, did not find any differences in attitudes based on locations of the institutions (see Table 4.13).

Many faculty members received their highest degree from Big Ten (81) or Ivy League (36) institutions. We could not distinguish between the two groups based on library attitudes (degrees of freedom: 115; two-tailed probability: .26). Perhaps graduate education has little influence on library attitudes. More likely, we suspect, graduate education at both groups of institutions resulted in similar attitudes about the library.

Discipline and Institution

We found it easy to believe that discipline-related experiences would highly influence faculty members. Holland's (1966) theory of vocational choice and personality espouses that individuals seek vocations that allow them to express their attitudes and values. According to Ladd and Lipset (1975a) in their major work, *The Divided Academy:*

> Within the university, a discipline's subject matter requires a bundle of professional work experiences, defines the groups and interests which serve as points of reference and association, and seems to attract people of a particular value orientation; together these factors contribute to the formation of distinctive discipline subcultures. (p. 69)

Even within the liberal arts college, Stark and Morstain (1978) found considerable diversity among the educational orientations of faculty members based on discipline. Therefore, we expected different library attitudes among the disciplines.

Our first test of this hypothesis confirmed our expectations (see Table 4.14). Significant differences did exist among the disciplines. Further analysis revealed that humanities faculty members held more positive attitudes

TABLE 4.14
ANOVA Summary Table by Attitudes and Disciplines

Source	Degrees of Freedom	Sum of Squares	Mean Squares	F Ratio	F Prob.
Between Groups	3	3,117.90	1,039.30	3.5	.015*
Among Groups	229	67,404.39	294.34		
Total	232	70,522.29			

*Significant at .05.

TABLE 4.15
Scheffe's Test of Attitudes and Disciplines

Discipline	Average Score	Fine Arts	Humanities	Social Sciences	Sciences
Fine Arts	136.5(13.3)				
Humanities	144.1(15.3)			*	
Sciences	136.4(19.2)		*		
Social Science	143.3(18.5)				

Note. Standard deviation in parenthesis.
*Denotes disciplines significantly different at the .1 level.

than the science faculty.[2] The fine arts faculty members held similar attitudes to the science faculty members, and the social science faculty members held similar attitudes to the humanities faculty members. The large standard deviations, however, showed considerable differences within each group (see Table 4.15).

We next examined the influence of institution. We expected from our own experiences, from the judges' selections, and from the literature that we would find considerable differences. We anticipated the most positive library attitudes from the Earlham faculty members. In turn, we expected the least positive library attitudes from the Purdue biology faculty. Again, our first analysis confirmed our expectations that differences did exist (see Table 4.16).

A further analysis showed that the Earlham faculty members had higher average scores than did the faculty members at the other institutions (see Table 4.17). In addition, the Purdue faculty members had lower average scores than did the other faculty members. The Evansville and Wabash faculty members expressed similar attitudes. We could not distinguish them from one another.

---

[2] We used the Scheffe's a posteriori contrast at the .1 level because of the conservative nature of the Scheffe's test (Kirk, 1968, pp. 95–97).

TABLE 4.16
ANOVA Summary Table by Attitudes and Institutions

Source	Degrees of Freedom	Sum of Squares	Mean Squares	F Ratio	F Prob.
Between Groups	3	11,815.06	3,938.35	15.4	.00
Among Groups	230	58,834.06	255.80		
Total	232	70,649.12			

TABLE 4.17
Scheffe's Test of Attitudes and Institutions

Institution	Average Score	Earlham	Evansville	Purdue	Wabash
Earlham	149.2(16.2)		*	*	*
Evansville	137.2(16.7)	*		*	
Purdue	126.4(17.3)	*	*		*
Wabash	140.9(13.8)	*		*	

Note. Standard deviation in parenthesis.
*Denotes disciplines significantly different at the .1 level.

TABLE 4.18
ANOVA Summary Table of Average Scores by Discipline within Institution

Source	Degrees of Freedom	Sum of Squares	Mean Squares	F Ratio	F Prob.
Between Groups	6	12,615.74	2,102.62	8.30	.00
Institution	3	9,497.98	3,165.99	12.66	.00
Discipline	3	783.21	261.07	1.04	.38
Interaction	6	2,463.94	410.66	1.60	.14
Residual	220	55,441.48	252.01		
Total	232	70,522.16	303.96		

We considered it possible that either institution or discipline is significant only because of its relationship with the other. Therefore, we conducted a two-way analysis of variance (see Table 4.18). Once we removed the influence of institution we could no longer distinguish among the attitudes based on discipline. In addition, the interaction of discipline and institution proved insignificant.

A further comparison emphasized the importance of institutional influences (see Table 4.19). The Earlham science faculty members included not only biology faculty members but also other science disciplines. Many of these disciplines, such as mathematics, physics, and chemistry, typically

TABLE 4.19
Average Attitude Scores Among Disciplines within Institutions

Institution	Average Score	Number at Institution
Earlham		
Fine Arts	142.0 (11.9)	7
Humanities	146.0 (16.5)	29
Sciences	155.8 (16.5)	18
Social Sciences	149.3 (15.7)	14
Evansville		
Fine Arts	133.7 (14.2)	17
Humanities	141.6 (13.5)	23
Sciences	130.1 (13.5)	16
Social Sciences	140.1 (21.3)	24
Purdue		
Sciences (Biology)	126.4 (17.3)	29
Wabash		
Fine Arts	138.0 (11.3)	6
Humanities	143.4 (15.4)	25
Sciences	138.9 (13.5)	17
Social Sciences	141.0 (11.8)	8
No Indication		1

Note. Standard deviation in parenthesis.

are not library-oriented at the undergraduate level. The Earlham science faculty members, however, had the highest average scores of all the groups. The Purdue faculty members, which included only biologists, had the lowest average scores. We conclude that institutional influences, not disciplinary, created the differences.

THE INTERVIEWS

From these findings and other evidence we conclude that local factors may highly shape library attitudes of faculty members. We noted both from our earlier visits and during our interviews that Earlham faculty members strongly supported the library's active role in undergraduate education. Such wide-spread views existed at no other institutions we either visited or surveyed.

From information gained from the interviews we can amplify the results of the survey and make other comparisons. In the interviews, faculty members often stated that student library use demanded too much faculty time. At the same time, most faculty members obviously worked hard to fulfill their teaching responsibilities. Often, we found they spent more time using other methods of teaching than library assignments would require.

Faculty members consider time of critical importance. They never have enough. With the continued expansion of knowledge, they chase infinity in trying to keep up with knowledge in their discipline. We found most emphasized the imparting of knowledge to students. Few, however, viewed the library as a way for students to learn how to gain this knowledge. Student library use is not a matter of time. It is a matter of values. Many faculty members we interviewed did not value the library's contribution to undergraduate education.

Few, however, openly stated this. Many had not thought much about the library. They responded only briefly to some of the questions. Some of their statements proved unclear, confusing, or meaningless to their colleagues. We tried to keep the statements in the original language from the interviews. After the reviews and the pilot test, we realized we had to revise the statements considerably for more faculty members to understand them.

For some areas, we could not draft useful attitude statements. Most of the faculty members, for example, seemed unable to express well-defined attitudes about library materials needed for undergraduate education (see Chapter Five). Some could not give a reason as to why they did not use the library in teaching undergraduates. Most had not given much thought to study conditions and other physical characteristics of the library. Very few referred to any educational philosophy or theory in discussing teaching practices. Only the Earlham faculty members clearly articulated a role for administrators in promoting undergraduate use of the library.

In fact, the Earlham faculty members, in contrast to the other faculty members, seemed to talk with their colleagues about teaching concerns. Faculty members at other institutions often seemed unaware of what each other did. They seldom alluded to discussions with their colleagues about teaching practices and philosophies. They appeared more to have formed their educational attitudes and practices through experience and reflection than through extensive discussions with their colleagues. Unlike Earlham, the other institutions do not have a strong tradition of team-teaching and interdisciplinary teaching.

Nevertheless, a few faculty members at the other institutions held attitudes similar to those held by most Earlham faculty members. These faculty members, however, seemed more isolated at their institutions than did any of the Earlham faculty. Some thought that within their department only they had their students use the library. In many ways Earlham College appeared distinctive, if not unique.

EARLHAM COLLEGE

What about Earlham College made its faculty members strongly support the library's integration into undergraduate education? First, Earlham College has a Quaker tradition. This tradition includes decision making by consensus. This facilitates the obvious spirit of cooperation among its faculty members, not obvious at the other institutions. Second, Earlham has a small and highly capable undergraduate enrollment. As with most small liberal arts colleges, it directs its primary mission at teaching undergraduates. These characteristics alone, however, do not explain Earlham's concentration on the library. We have other small liberal arts Quaker institutions. Even within this study, Wabash College had a small and equally capable undergraduate enrollment. Yet, these other institutions have not exhibited the same use of the library as did Earlham.

The long tenure of a very capable library director, Evan Farber, partially explained Earlham's situation. Farber has both the respect of his library and faculty colleagues at Earlham and the national recognition given him by librarians. Largely through his efforts, Earlham College maintains well-funded and well-staffed libraries. Farber strongly supports the public services aspects of librarianship, particularly bibliographic instruction. He, personally, provides many, if not most, of the bibliographic instruction sessions. In addition, he retains able librarians and support staff.

Still, we must look even further for a more complete explanation of Earlham's extensive library use. During the interviews, Earlham's faculty members emphasized that Earlham College, in fact, took seriously its stated commitment to undergraduates. Hiring practices, it became clear, emphasized faculty members' abilities to teach and to fit into the Earlham "experience." Both librarians and faculty members at Earlham stressed that the institution awarded tenure not on a good research and publishing record alone. Faculty members could "publish and perish" at Earlham if they did not teach well. Some untenured faculty members commented on a strong institutional expectation that they should involve the library in their teaching. They found encouragement from several directions to adapt to the Earlham "experience."

Significantly, almost half of the Earlham faculty did not have tenure (see Table 4.4), a much higher percentage than any of the other institutions. We suspect Earlham's hiring practices, new faculty orientations, and tenure policies countered any tendencies of new faculty members toward the "university-library syndrome."

In addition, Earlham had a very active faculty development program. This program bolstered Earlham's norm of team-teaching and interdisciplinary teaching. It encouraged the discussions among the faculty members we already mentioned. Faculty members seemed to trust one another. This same tradition of sharing one's classroom with a faculty member colleague probably encouraged the sharing of one's classroom with a librarian. In fact, some faculty members referred to the librarians as faculty even though the librarians do not have formal faculty status. When we pointed this out to faculty members, they stated that the Earlham faculty members considered the librarians as members of the faculty.

Not only did Earlham's faculty members trust each other, they trusted in their administrators. When asked, they readily provided extensive, articulate answers about roles administrators could play about the library. At the other institutions, the faculty members responded in one of three ways. Often they could not think of a role for the administrators. Sometimes they expressed resentment that administrators might encourage a particular method of teaching. Occasionally, upon some reflection they stated that administrators could provide more money for the library. In later discussions of the various factors of library attitudes, the reader will see how positive attitudes toward administrators strongly identified Earlham's faculty members.

Finally, Earlham's librarians, faculty members, and administrators all expressed a strong belief about Earlham being "special." Perhaps every institution has some feeling of distinctiveness. When as widely and deeply held as at Earlham, it perpetuates institutional norms. Annual bibliographic instruction workshops, addresses by faculty members at regional and national conferences, and a steady stream of visitors to the campus all carefully cultivated a dedication to the library's involvement in undergraduate education. Through various means, Earlham's librarians, faculty members, and administrators have given public testimony to their commitment to the library. Through this testimony they have shared with each other their attitudes toward the library and increased their commitment. Diverse elements of the academic community carefully nurtured the Earlham "experience," including the library's role in it.

CONCLUSIONS

We believe that many faculty members have limited views about the library's role in undergraduate education. Our conclusion, however, should not discourage librarians. We also conclude that local conditions, more so than previous experiences, influence the faculty member's attitudes toward the library. Within their own institutions, librarians can make a difference. At Earlham College, for example, several conditions created by the librarians favored the library's integration into undergraduate education.

To make a difference, however, librarians need to understand the complexities of faculty culture. Librarians need a broad understanding of the faculty's perspective. This understanding will help allow librarians to move beyond the confines of the library and to work with individual faculty members. Our findings challenge librarians because we do not believe that attitudes of faculty members are unalterably shaped by their graduate school experience. The "university-library syndrome" does exist. We, however, optimistically believe that with increased knowledge librarians successfully can overcome traditional attitudes toward the library.

chapter five

DIMENSIONS OF LIBRARY ATTITUDES

INTRODUCTION

We report in this chapter our examination through factor analysis of the interrelationships among the responses to the attitude statements. Often several dimensions or factors make up a construct. For example, psychologists have shown what we call intelligence includes verbal ability, numerical ability, abstract reasons, spatial reasoning, memory, and other elements (Kerlinger, 1973). Therefore, we assumed that the *Library Educational Attitudes Scale* (LEAS) included several underlying dimensions or factors.

EXPLORATORY FACTOR ANALYSIS

Hypothesis testing guides confirmatory factor analysis. "Hunches or simply an open question about the number and kinds of factors which might be derivable from a collection of variables" (Nunnally, 1978, p. 331), however, guides exploratory factor analysis. Exploratory factor analysis allowed us to explore "the underlying factor structure without prior specifications of number of factors or their loadings" (Kim & Mueller, 1978, p. 77). It condensed the variables into a relatively small number of factors. This helped us to identify and to interpret the basic properties of the attitude scale. Each factor consisted of a cluster of statements that correlated highly with each other and correlated lowly with other clusters of statements (Nunnally, 1978).

We analyzed the field test results through the FACTOR subprogram of version 8.1 of *SPSS* with the PA2 (principal factoring with interaction) and VARIMAX orthogonal procedures. Researchers commonly use these procedures in exploratory factor analysis. These procedures increase the differences in any factor structure underlying the data (Nunnally, 1978). That is, they organized the data to prevent any one statement from loading on more than one factor.

TABLE 5.1
Initial Factor Analysis of LEAS

Factor	Eigenvalue	Percent of Total Variance	Cumulative Percent of Total Variance
1	4.89	16.3	16.3
2	2.77	9.2	25.5
3	1.89	6.3	31.8
4	1.62	5.4	37.2
5	1.54	5.1	42.3
6	1.25	4.2	46.5
7	1.19	4.0	50.5
8	1.11	3.7	54.2
9	1.06	3.5	57.7
10	1.00	3.4	61.0

Note. Values are prior to rotation.

Initial Factor Analysis

The initial factor analysis before rotation revealed 10 factors with eigenvalues over 1.0. These factors accounted for 61 percent of the variance in the data (see Table 5.1). The variance explained by each factor, as shown by the eigenvalue, significantly dropped after five factors. Therefore, the scree test suggested the extraction of five factors for further analysis (Cattell, 1966).

The scree test is a rule-of-thumb criterion. We could have used it to determine the number of factors to extract based on the point where the large eigenvalue drop occurred. The scree test, however, works best when we have prior knowledge of the factors and can extract many variables for every factor (Gorsuch, 1974). Lacking either of these conditions, we used a more acceptable method. We limited the number of factors extracted to those with eigenvalues greater than one (Rummel, 1970). Ten factors had eigenvalues at 1.0 or above.

We wanted the average loading on each factor significantly high so we could have confidence that the factor existed beyond our particular respondents (Nunnally, 1978). When we analyzed the factor loadings of these 10 factors, only four factors proved nontrivial (see Table 5.2). That is, only four factors had four or more statements loading on them at .3 or above.

The reader may want an explanation of our criteria for assigning statements to individual factors and for determining the meaningfulness of factors. We have no universally accepted standard of error of factor loadings (Kerlinger, 1973). Nevertheless, the factor loadings are like correlations and we interpreted them similarly (Kerlinger, 1973). Some researchers recommended use of the standard error of a correlation matrix to deter-

TABLE 5.2
First Varimax Rotated Factor Matrix Nontrivial Factors

Statement	Factor 1	Factor 2	Factor 3	Factor 4	Communalities[a]
1	.63*	.27	.06	−.14	.45
2	.06	.43*	.34	−.17	.36
3	.25	.42*	.29	−.09	.37
4	−.13	−.30*	−.15	.19	.39
5	.18	.66*	.03	.07	.39
6	−.10	−.09	−.05	.34*	.27
7	−.17	−.01	−.01	.04	.23
8	−.05	−.04	.01	.68*	.36
9	.09	−.35*	−.21	.31	.32
10	.12	.54*	.06	−.07	.33
11	−.15	−.10	.21	.45*	.35
12	−.36	−.10	.06	.37*	.43
13	.23	.11	.48*	.13	.30
14	−.20	−.10	.04	.03	.24
15	.08	−.03	−.21	−.21	.19
16	−.06	−.35*	.13	.13	.26
17	.72*	.00	.11	−.12	.50
18	−.27	.18	−.11	.32*	.27
19	.14	.05	.40*	−.06	.22
20	−.17	−.19	.22	.23	.27
21	−.06	−.03	.06	.11	.19
22	−.30*	−.24	.24	.01	.40
23	−.07	−.19	.13	.16	.38
24	−.08	−.04	.57*	.10	.33
25	−.07	.06	.06	.06	.18
26	.18	−.26	−.06	.38*	.34
27	.40*	.19	.35	−.06	.42
28	.10	.18	.56*	.03	.41
29	.53*	.20	.14	.03	.50
30	.04	−.03	.26	.05	.25
Eigenvalue	4.89	2.77	1.89	1.61	9.6/11.16
Percent of Total Variance	16.33	9.2	6.3	5.4	Total 37.2
Percent of Common Variance	43.8	24.8	16.9	14.4	

Note. The factor loading can be interpreted as the correlation coefficient between each item and the underlying factors. The eigenvalues equal the sum of the column of squared loadings for each factor in the unrotated matrix and measure the amount of variation accounted for by a factor. The percent of total variance is a measure of the variation among all the variables involved in a particular factor as a percentage of the total variation of the unrotated data matrix. The percent of common variance is a measure of the variation among all variables involved in a particular factor as a percentage of that involved in all factors.
[a]Communality measures the proportion of variation of each item involved in the factor. Communalities and eigenvalues are from the unrotated matrix.
*Items loading on factor at .3 or above and higher than on any other factor.

mine the loading of items on a factor (Kerlinger, 1973; Nunnally, 1978). For this study, we have a correlation as low as .15 significant beyond the .01 level for a population of 234. Therefore, we could assign statements with factor loadings significant at the .01 level to a factor (Kerlinger, 1973).

We, however, also considered the recommendations of other research-ers. Kim and Mueller (1978) considered the .3 level as a rule of thumb for the assignment of meaningful statements to a factor. Gorsuch (1974) considered nontrivial those factors with at least two or three factors load-ing above .3. Therefore, we assigned the attitude statements to the factor on which they had the highest loading at .3 or above.

Also, the amount of variance accounted for by a factor relates to number of items in a scale (eigenvalue divided by number of items equals percent of total variance). Therefore, factors with eigenvalues as small as the tradi-tional cutoff point of 1.0 contributed little to the variance of the data ma-trix. They also did not have enough number of items loading at .3 or above to be meaningful and interpretable. Using these criteria, we extracted four factors (see Table 5.2) with eigenvalues well above 1.0. All have at least four attitude statements loading on them at .3 or above.

Final Factor Analysis

A second factor analysis forced the extraction of the four factors (see Table 5.3). Note that the rotated factors explained the same amount of variance as the original factors. They, however, divided the variance differently to aid interpretation. We assigned attitude statements to the factor on which they had the highest loading at .3 or above. Four attitude statements exhib-ited similar equal loadings on two or more factors. We assigned those state-ments to the factor that seemed most conceptually appropriate.

Statements 15, 21, and 25 also correlated with the total scale score at an insignificant level (see Appendix A, Table A.3). Therefore, they did not contribute meaningfully to the variance of the scale. The low communali-ties of statements 15, 21, and 25 provided additional support for the lack of any meaningful contribution.[1]

Item 15 states, "Librarians should have advanced degrees in other disci-plines in addition to a degree in library science if they are to help students use the library." About 45 percent of the faculty members disagreed and about 30 percent agreed with this statement. About one-quarter of the faculty members, however, responded neutrally (see Appendix A, Table

---

[1] Communality provides a measure of the order, uniformity, and regularity in the data (Rummel, 1972, p. 45). The communality times 100 gives the percent of variation of a state-ment in common with the total scale. When the percent of variation is substracted from one hundred, it gives a measure of the uniqueness of the statement.

TABLE 5.3
Varimax Rotated Factor Matrix Final Four Factors

Statement	Factor 1	Factor 2	Factor 3	Factor 4	Communalities
1	.54*	.29	.18	−.11	.45
2	−.06	.50*	.30	−.15	.36
3	.18	.35*	.34	−.25	.37
4	−.27	−.45*	−.07	.13	.39
5	.11	.69*	.07	.18	.39
6	−.25	−.09	−.03	.45*	.27
7	−.33*	−.06	−.04	.18	.23
8	−.05	−.10	.07	.52*	.36
9	.02	−.43*	−.09	.33	.32
10	.02	.50*	.13	−.15	.33
11	−.20	−.11	.16	.45*	.35
12	−.47*	−.23	.08	.36	.43
13	.07	.10	.50*	.14	.30
14	−.35*	−.21	.05	−.03	.24
15	.23	−.10	−.14	−.00	.19
16	−.17	−.21	−.01	.19	.26
17	.66*	.13	.16	−.06	.50
18	−.32	.02	−.01	.33*	.27
19	.08	.10	.43*	−.03	.22
20	−.12	−.26	.29	.22	.27
21	−.01	−.03	.15	.16	.19
22	−.37*	−.31	.19	.14	.40
23	−.13	−.35*	.21	.30	.38
24	−.20	−.04	.52*	.10	.33
25	−.06	.05	.13	.06	.18
26	.17	−.08	−.05	.54*	.34
27	.30	.11	.47*	−.13	.42
28	.10	.15	.60*	−.08	.41
29	.66*	.27	.23	.07	.50
30	.08	−.03	.32*	.01	.25
Eigenvalue	4.89	2.77	1.89	1.61	9.6/11.16
Percent of Total Variance	16.33	9.2	6.3	5.4	Total 37.2
Percent of Common Variance	50.0	24.3	14.5	11.3	

*Items loading on factor at .3 or above and higher than on any other factor.

A-2). From both the item-total correlation and the factor analysis, we concluded this question did not draw upon library educational attitudes, as defined in this study. Perhaps most faculty members do not have established attitudes about this issue. The question could have appeared unclear if they had not thought about the subject.

Item 16 states, "My students should use the library to learn how scholars examine major works and ideas in my discipline." The responses to this question did correlate significantly with the total scale score. Using the minimum significance level (.15), we could have assigned it to one of three factors. It, however, did not load at the .3 level or above on any factor. Therefore, it did not provide a strong contribution to the interpretation of any of them.

Item 20 states, "I should evaluate the library assignments of my students on the same basis as any other assignment for my courses." This statement barely missed the assignment cutoff point of .29. A fairly large percentage (16.2) of the faculty members also responded neutrally. While contributing to the total attitude scale, it did not give strong meaning to any one factor.

Item 21 states, "The small college library should satisfy the library needs of my undergraduate students just as adequately as the large university library." The faculty members seemed divided about this question but not neutral. Whatever attitude domain this question drew upon, it did not measure the same attitudes as the rest of the scale. It neither correlated significantly with the total scale score nor loaded sufficiently on any of the factors.

Item 25 states, "Student frustration in using the library should be considered a normal part of learning how to use the library." Some interviewed faculty members made this statement. It, however, had little meaning to their surveyed colleagues in relation to other library attitudes. It neither correlated with the total attitude scale score nor loaded sufficiently on any of the four factors.

Comparison With Other Procedures

As we stated earlier, the Varimax procedure emphasized any underlying factors and reduced the depiction of any general factor. The Oblique rotation method, which simplified factors, also revealed very similar factors (see Table 5.4). We have provided eigenvalues for unrotated factors. After orthogonal rotation, one can not attach significance to factor order (Rummel, 1972).

We imposed orthogonality through the Varimax rotation, that is, rotation to downplay factor intercorrelation. Oblique rotation does not impose orthogonality. Nevertheless, the Oblique factor structure depicted a high degree of orthogonality. When we included with a factor only the highest loading statements of .3 or above, both the Oblique and Varimax factors intercorrelated. We should expect factors constructed from only the highest loading statements (which enhances understanding) to have some significant intercorrelation (see Table 5.5).

TABLE 5.4
Comparison of Varimax and Oblique Rotation Methods

Factors	Varimax One	Oblique Three	Varimax Two	Oblique One
*Statements	1	1	2	2
	7		3	
	12	12	4	4
	14	14	5	5
	17	17	9	9
	22		10	10
	29	29	23	23
Eigenvalues	4.89	1.88	2.77	4.89
Factors	**Three**	**Two**	**Four**	**Four**
*Statements		3	6	6
	13	13	8	8
	19	19	11	11
		20	18	18
	24	24	26	26
	28	28		
	30	30		
Eigenvalues	1.89	2.77	1.61	1.61

Note. Eigenvalues are from unrotated matrix.
*Statements loading on factors at .3 or above and higher than on any other factor.

   Intercorrelation necessarily may not be a problem in understanding the factors. Many conceptually independent variables, such as height and weight or verbal and mathematical ability, correlate. Nunnally recommended a test of the confidence in a variable. He used the average correlation among the variables hypothesized to form a particular factor. We compared this average with the standard error of a correlation matrix. We found the average correlations among the items on each factor above the level of significance (see Table 5.6). Therefore, we can have confidence that the factors existed beyond the faculty members included in this study (Nunnally, 1978). Nunnally described this test as "a highly conservative rule of thumb" (p. 421).

Interpreting the Four Factors

We did have some overlap among the four factors and redundancy in predicting the total score. The four factors, however, added to the understanding of the composition of library educational attitudes. Strictly speaking, faculty members probably hold attitudes related to each of the factors uncovered. Nevertheless, for the sake of clarity and understanding, we discuss

TABLE 5.5
Factor Correlation Matrices

Varimax Factors	Factor One	Factor Two	Factor Three	Factor Four
Factor One				
Factor Two	.50			
Factor Three	.25	.32		
Factor Four	.40	.28	.07*	
Total[a]	.52	.54	.28	.38

Oblique Factor Structure	Factor One	Factor Two	Factor Three	Factor Four
Factor One				
Factor Two	−.15*			
Factor Three	−.18	.01*		
Factor Four	.30	.09*	−.20	

Oblique Factors	Factor One	Factor Two	Factor Three	Factor Four
Factor One				
Factor Two	.37			
Factor Three	.51	.37		
Factor Four	.28	.17	.38	
Total[a]	.53	.41	.54	.38

Note. Factors only include statements that loaded .3 or above and highest on that particular factor; negative statements recoded.
[a]Individual factor score removed from total score to avoid misleading high correlation through self-correlation.
*Not significant at .01 level.

the factors as they related to faculty members *strongly* associated with a particular factor.

Factor One: Library-resistance Faculty Members.
This factor correlated significantly with the total scale score (see Table 5.5) and had a high internal consistency—even across institutions (see Table 5.7). It both explained a moderate amount of the variance of the scale and "held together." That is, the responses to the statements intercorrelated (see Appendix A for a more complete explanation).

Faculty members who scored high on this factor resisted any involvement with the library in their undergraduate teaching. In a sense, they appeared to absolve themselves from any responsibility for the library. They held the attitude that librarians, not themselves, should teach undergraduates how to use the library. They disagreed that they should develop assignments to introduce students to the library. They did not see it as an unfavorable reflection on themselves or their department if their undergraduates did not use the library. At all levels of undergraduates, they considered subject content more important to teach than the development of library skills. They believed, as did the faculty members described by Colorado College President Riley, the "mastery of the library to be an easy task" (1984, p. 12).

We found significant differences (see Table 5.8) among the faculty members by institution in the responses to this factor. Table 5.9 shows that the Purdue biological science faculty members scored significantly lower than the Earlham and Wabash faculty. Earlham faculty members scored significantly higher than the Evansville and Purdue faculty members. (We recoded the items to signify low scores as negative responses.) The Purdue faculty members most closely identified with this factor. The Earlham faculty members least closely identified with it.

Factor Two: Library-minimization Faculty Members.
This factor correlated at a moderate level with both the total scale score and with factor one (see Table 5.5). It also had a high internal consistency across institutions (see Table 5.7). Faculty members who scored high on this factor, unlike the library-resistant faculty members, conceded at least a minimal role for the library in undergraduate education. Nevertheless, they expected only the brightest students to use the library. For most of their students, the library served largely as a study hall. These faculty members seemed both unwilling to become familiar with the library resources and to help students use the library.

Similarly to the faculty members strongly identified with factor one, these faculty members expressed little concern about the use of library collections. They held that needed library proficiency consisted only of the skills needed to use the card catalog. Riley (1984) supported the existence of faculty members associated with this factor when he described those who believed, "Extensive use of the library is only for the brightest; for the rest, it is merely a study hall" (p. 13).

Table 5.10 shows a significant difference existed among the faculty members by institution as to their responses to this factor. Table 5.11 shows that the Purdue faculty members scored less positively on this factor than the other faculty members. We did not find a distinction among the other faculty members.

Factor Three: Library-traditionalist Faculty Members.
This factor correlated at a moderate level with the total scale score and with factors one and two but not significantly with factor four (see Table 5.5). It only had modest internal consistency across the four institutions

TABLE 5.6
Library Educational Attitudes Scale: Individual Factors

FACTOR ONE: LIBRARY-RESISTANCE	Factor Loading	Item/Factor Correlation[a]
Reliability Coefficients: .73		
29. I should be able to leave to librarians the responsibility of teaching students how to use the library.	.66	.52
17. Teaching additional content in my upper-level courses should be more important than spending time teaching my students how to use the library.	.66	.59
1. Teaching additional content in my lower-level courses should be more important than spending time teaching my students how to use the library.	.54	.58
12. I should develop an interesting problem or quest to introduce my students to the library.	− .47	.50
22. It should reflect poorly on my department if the library is not heavily used by students in our courses.	− .37	.33
14. I should have the main responsibility for ensuring that my students make good use of the library.	− .33	.24
FACTOR TWO: LIBRARY-MINIMIZATION		
Reliability Coefficient: .70		
5. Assignments requiring students to use the library demand too much of my time in relation to my other responsibilities.	.69	.44
2. I should expect only my brightest students to make good use of the library collections.	.50	.45
10. For students in my courses, the library should be considered primarily as a place to study textbooks, lecture notes, and similar materials.	.50	.48
4. I should help my students develop the ability to use the literature of my discipline in the library.	− .45	.45
9. I should be familiar with the range of library resources useful in teaching my students.	− .43	.43
23. I should be concerned if the library collection in my discipline is little used.	− .35	.28
3. A knowledge of how to use the card catalog should be sufficient familiarity with the library for students to use it for my courses.	.35	.43

TABLE 5.6   (Continued)
Library Educational Attitudes Scale: Individual Factors

FACTOR THREE: LIBRARY-TRADITIONALIST	Factor Loading	Item/Factor Correlation[a]
Reliability Coefficient: .59		
28. Administrators should seek to admit a high proportion of very capable students if they want me to require my students to use the library.	.60	.49
24. Administrators should ensure small classes to encourage me to require my students to use the library.	.52	.32
13. The size of the library collections in my discipline should serve as measure of how well the library will serve the needs of my students.	.47	.20
19. The library should be quiet to encourage my students to use it.	.43	.37
30. Being surrounded by books in the library should have a positive influence on students whether they use them or not.	.32	.24
FACTOR FOUR: LIBRARY-ACTIVE		
Reliability Coefficient: .60		
26. Librarians should help me by teaching my students how to use the library.	.54	.26
8. Administrators should promote the view that librarians are full partners with me in the educational process.	.52	.42
6. My students should have specific instructions on how to use the library in each course in which I require its use.	.45	.37
11. Administrators should take a leadership role in encouraging students to use the library.	.45	.44
18. I should be better prepared to teach students how to make good use of the library.	.33	.29

[a]Negative statements recoded for a positive correlation with a total factor score. All statements correlated significantly at the .01 level with the assigned total factor score. Individual statements were removed from the factor score to avoid a misleading correlation through self-correlation.

(see Table 5.7). Faculty members who scored high on this factor expressed what we called "traditional attitudes" toward the library's role in undergraduate education.

They measured the adequacy of the library by the *size* of the collections. These faculty members, however, expressed little concern about the use of

TABLE 5.7
Reliability Coefficients by Factor and Institution

	Factor One	Factor Two	Factor Three	Factor Four	Total
Earlham	.75	.71	.52	.62	.76
Evansville	.63	.72	.49	.60	.77
Purdue	.69	.61	.61	.54	.77
Wabash	.78	.63	.66	.35	.70
Total for Each Factor	.73	.70	.59	.60	
Total Scale Reliability Coefficient					.79

TABLE 5.8
ANOVA Summary Table of Factor One Attitude Scores Among Institutions

Source	Degrees of Freedom	Sum of Squares	Mean Squares	F Ratio	F Prob.
Between Groups	3	1,095.53	365.18	7.9	.00
Among Groups	230	10,748.51	46.73		
Total	233	11,844.05			

Note. Reject the null hypothesis of no differences among the institutions.

TABLE 5.9
Scheffe's Test of Factor One Attitudes Among Institutions

Institution	Average Score	Earlham	Evansville	Purdue	Wabash
Earlham	30.29 (7.2)		*	*	
Evansville	26.57 (6.4)	*			
Purdue	23.21 (6.4)	*			*
Wabash	27.60 (7.1)			*	

Note. Standard deviations in parentheses.
*Denotes institutions significantly different at the .1 level.

these collections. They expected library use only by the more capable students. As with the faculty members associated with the previous two factors, these faculty members considered the library easy for undergraduates to learn how to use.

For these faculty members, administrators do have a role in encouraging use of the library. For these faculty members, administrators should not

TABLE 5.10
ANOVA Summary Table of Factor Two Attitude Scores Among Institutions

Source	Degrees of Freedom	Sum of Squares	Mean Squares	F Ratio	F Prob.
Between Groups	3	599.01	199.67	7.3	.00
Among Groups	230	6,249.64	27.17		
Total	233	6,848.64			

Note. Reject the null hypothesis of no differences among the institutions.

TABLE 5.11
Scheffe's Test of Factor Two Attitudes Among Institutions

Institution	Average Score	Earlham	Evansville	Purdue	Wabash
Earlham	41.93 (5.5)			*	
Evansville	40.42 (5.3)			*	
Purdue	36.69 (5.7)	*	*		*
Wabash	41.36 (4.3)			*	

Note. Standard deviations in parentheses.
*Denotes institutions significantly different at the .1 level

directly encourage use of the library. They, however, should attract highly capable students to the institution. Administrators should then make sure these students can enroll in small classes. Only students in these classes need to use the library.

Overall, these faculty members considered the library's role passive. It should be a quiet place to study. Just having books, lots of books, positively influences students. Students, however, do not necessarily need to read these books. Many faculty members during the interviews described the library as a place that invited students to learn. These faculty members considered it very important that libraries displayed book jackets, offered poetry readings, and, in general, celebrated the book. They, however, seldom mentioned any structured efforts to introduce students to the intricacies of the library. Inspiration, for them, took precedence over direction in getting students to use the library.

Knapp (1958) also identified these faculty members in her studies. Her faculty members believed only in small classes could they give the individual attention to students needed to guide and stimulate use of the library. Only potential graduate students needed a high level of library competence.

An analysis of variance test (see Table 5.12) shows a significant differ-

TABLE 5.12
ANOVA Summary Table of Factor Three Attitude Scores Among Institutions

Source	Degrees of Freedom	Sum of Squares	Mean Squares	F Ratio	F Prob.
Between Groups	3	727.52	242.51	7.9	.00
Among Groups	230	7,041.13	30.61		
Total	233	7,768.65			

Note. Reject the null hypothesis of no differences among the institutions.

ence among the mean score on this factor among the faculty members according to institution. A Scheffe's test (see Table 5.13) shows that the Purdue faculty members scored lower on this factor than Wabash's or Earlham's faculty members. The Evansville's faculty members scored lower than Earlham's faculty members. We found no differences between the scores of the faculty members from the two liberal arts colleges.

Factor Four: Library-active Faculty Members.
This factor correlated at a moderate level with the total attitude score and with factors one and two but not with factor three (see Table 5.5). It had a moderate internal consistency across three of four of the institutions. Its low coefficient at Wabash suggested that it is not a well-defined factor among faculty members at that institution (see Table 5.7).

Faculty members who scored high on this factor supported the active involvement of the library in undergraduate education. They believed specific instructions are necessary to teach students how to use the library. They expressed concern about their own preparation to teach students how to use the library. These faculty members declared a willingness to share this responsibility with librarians. In fact, they looked at librarians as *full* partners in the educational process.

TABLE 5.13
Scheffe's Test of Factor Three Attitudes among Institutions

Institution	Average Score	Earlham	Evansville	Purdue	Wabash
Earlham	26.39 (5.1)		*	*	
Evansville	23.17 (5.4)	*			
Purdue	21.21 (6.0)	*			*
Wabash	25.60 (5.9)			*	

Note. Standard deviations in parentheses.
*Denotes institutions significantly different at the .1 level.

TABLE 5.14
ANOVA Summary Table of Factor Four Attitude Scores among Institutions

Source	Degrees of Freedom	Sum of Squares	Mean Squares	F Ratio	F Prob.
Between Groups	3	698.56	232.85	10.7	.00
Among Groups	230	5,019.27	21.82		
Total	233	5,717.83			

Note. Reject the null hypothesis of no differences among the institutions.

Their attitudes toward administrators represented the key to this factor. Faculty members strongly associated with this factor not only recognized a role for administrators, but a leadership role. During the interviews, only members of the Earlham faculty expressed such support for administrators. In fact, we had almost given up asking questions about the administrators. Not that we received negative responses to this question, we usually did not receive any responses. Most faculty members had not thought about an active role of administrators in encouraging students to use the library.

The Wabash faculty members we interviewed maintained, "We don't have any administrators." For them, this meant that everyone, including the president, taught classes. Nevertheless, this statement also reflected a certain distaste for administrative responsibilities and administrators. In the eyes of many faculty members, administrators served best as facilitators to help the faculty members to do what they wanted to do. In this role, administrators could help by "providing more money to the library." When asked about a more active role, some interviewees responded that administrators "should stay out of the way." We did not find this view at Earlham College.

An analysis of variance test (see Table 5.14) shows a significant difference among the average scores on this factor according to institutions. A Scheffe's test (see Table 5.15) shows that the Earlham faculty members scored higher on this factor than any of the other faculty members. In fact, from the Scheffe's test, we could not find any differences among the average scores of the other faculty members. Attitudes expressed by this factor remained most characteristic of the Earlham faculty members. We did, however, find some individual faculty members at the other institutions who supported these attitudes.

SUMMARY AND CONCLUSIONS

In this chapter we reported on the analysis of the various factors or dimensions of the Library Education Attitude Scale (LEAS). We sought through

TABLE 5.15
Scheffe's Test of Factor Four Attitudes Among Institutions

Institution	Average Score	Earlham	Evansville	Purdue	Wabash
Earlham	27.29 (4.5)		*	*	*
Evansville	23.85 (4.9)	*			
Purdue	22.79 (5.1)	*			
Wabash	23.53 (4.1)	*			

Note. Standard deviations in parentheses.
*Denotes institutions significantly different at the .1 level.

exploratory factor analysis further understanding of the relationships among variables. We found the LEAS consisted of four identifiable dimensions. These dimensions or factors met the necessary psychometric criteria to show their validity and reliability. In addition, we found information in the literature to bolster futher claims of their existence. Therefore, we found them useful to gain further insights into the differences among faculty members' library attitudes.

We discovered, not unexpectedly, faculty members dissimilar in their attitudes towards library. While they responded moderately positively overall, the faculty members reported a full range of positive and negative attitudes. We identified faculty members at specific institutions with particular dimensions of the scale. The Earlham faculty members supported an active role for the library. The Purdue biological science faculty members viewed the library as a passive institution. The Wabash and Evansville faculty members, however, seemed divided.

This analysis provided more understanding to the responses to individual questions. For example, when library-resistance faculty members agreed with statement 29, "I should be able to leave to librarians the responsibility of teaching students how to use the library," they did not express strong confidence in the teaching abilities of librarians. Instead, they held library skills inconsequential (Statement 7). Such skills could be safely assign to librarians to teach. These faculty members then could concentrate on what they considered more important, that is, the content of their discipline (Statements 1 and 17).

On the other hand, library-active faculty members perceived a need (Statement 6) for these skills. Yet, they felt some inadequacy in teaching them (Statement 18). As colleagues (Statement 8), librarians could help (Statement 27) faculty members teach students needed library skills. When viewed in this context, these faculty members obviously held a much different view of library skills and librarians than did the library-resistance faculty members.

These factors are not altogether distinct entities within the scale. Individuals frequently hold interrelated and overlapping, and sometimes contradictory attitudes. If we view individual faculty members only as library-resistance, minimization, traditionalist, or active, we overgeneralize. Nevertheless, these dimensions do provide further insights into the referents faculty members use in judging the library's undergraduate education role.

chapter six

SELECTING LIBRARY MATERIALS FOR UNDERGRADUATES*

INTRODUCTION

In this chapter we report our efforts to determine the faculty members' attitudes toward library materials suitable for undergraduates. Librarians, students, administrators, and faculty members alike support the acquisition of library materials for instruction, research, and other needs. Each group shares in this responsibility. Faculty members, nonetheless, have a dominant role. Without their requirements, we would not have the academic library as we know it today. They largely determine both the amount and type of undergraduate use of library materials. Among colleges, faculty members select a great deal, if not most, of the materials acquired annually for the library. Students of academia, however, have conducted little empirical research about attitudes of faculty members in this area. We found our foray into this realm rather baffling.

BACKGROUND

Librarians have long recognized the specific library needs of undergraduates. Wagman (1956) traced their concerns for undergraduates' library needs back to 1608 with the appointment of Thomas James to Bodley's library. In his new position, James suggested setting up an undergraduate library to help the younger students. Sir Thomas Bodley, however, rejected the proposal. Three and a half centuries later, universities began following James's advice. Beginning with Harvard's Lamont Library, several large universities set up separate undergraduate libraries during the post-World War II period. In addition, at the hundreds of primarily undergraduate

---

* Portions of this chapter were previously published as Hardesty, L. (1986, March). Book Selection for Undergraduates: A Study of Faculty Attitudes. *The Journal of Academic Librarianship, 12,* 19–25.

institutions, libraries continued to strive to serve the needs of undergraduates.

Dating from Shaw's *A List of Books for College Libraries* (1931), librarians and others have compiled lists to aid in the book selection for undergraduate libraries. The post-World War II period saw the development of the Lamont list (McNiff, 1953), the Michigan list (*Undergraduate Library*, 1964), and the California list (Voigt & Treyz, 1967). More recently, we have *Choice's Opening Day Collection* (Gardner, 1974) and the second and third editions of *Books for College Libraries* (ACRL, 1975, 1988). In addition, several lists in specific subject areas aid book selection for undergraduate libraries.

Lists soon become dated and lose their usefulness. In the early 1960s the American Library Association, through a grant from the Council on Library Resources, established *Choice* as a current review service of books for undergraduate libraries. *Choice* now includes 6,600 reviews annually. Typically, the reviewer makes a distinction about the level or levels for which he or she considers the book appropriate. The reviewer may recommend the book for libraries serving lower-level undergraduate students, upper-level undergraduate students, graduate students, or all level of students.

Several reasons exist for acquisition of materials for the academic library. Cline and Sinnott (1981), in their study of the development of academic library collections, listed six motives:

1. Support of a basic liberal arts curriculum
2. Support of a specific undergraduate curriculum
3. Support of a graduate or professional training program
4. Support of a continuing education or an extension program
5. Maintenance of a reference collection
6. Maintenance of a research collection, which can range from minimal to comprehensive.

They found these neither necessarily well-defined nor mutually exclusive groups. A library may acquire an item with several purposes in mind or acquire it for one purpose and later maintain it for another.

How well can materials selectors discriminate among the different levels of library materials and reasons for selecting them for the academic library? In particular, how well can faculty members discriminate between materials suitable for the undergraduate library and those that are not? Do faculty members have well-defined and widely held criteria for selecting materials for the undergraduate library? On which characteristics of materials do faculty members base their recommendations? Is it the vocabulary, the complexity of the expression of ideas, the details of the documentation, the accuracy of the information, or some other characteristic or combination of characteristics? We sought to answer these questions in our study.

Many faculty members and librarians may share Danton's (1963) view, who wrote, "Faculty participation in book selection is the major asset of current American policy and practice" (p. 82). Lyle (1974), however, has pointed out, "There is very little factual information on the methods by which faculty go about choosing library materials" (p. 177). We cannot simply state that materials selection is up to the preferences or judgments of individual faculty members. We cannot accept this as an answer as how to select library materials for undergraduates. This answer tells nothing about how librarians can use those criteria to help faculty make better selections.

RESULTS FROM THIS STUDY

We tried in this study to determine faculty's attitudes toward the types of materials suitable for the undergraduate library. In our interviews we included the following two general questions:

1. What kinds of collections do you need in the library for undergraduates?
2. Can a small college library serve undergraduates in your discipline as adequately as a large research library can? Please explain your answer.

We used these questions to open the discussion of undergraduate library materials. A series of more specific questions followed. For example, we asked how they selected library materials for use by undergraduates. We asked them to describe the differences in their discipline between library materials appropriate for undergraduates and those appropriate for graduate students.

As we explained earlier, from these interviews, a review of the literature, and personal experience, we drafted 130 attitude statements. We used the original language of the faculty members as much as possible. We then dropped repetitious and obviously ambiguous statements until 90 statements remained. Next, 12 judges, 6 librarians, and 6 faculty members reviewed the statements. After their review, we cut another 20 statements. Another 6 judges reviewed these statements, and we reduced the statements to 60. We then tested the 60 statements in a Likert-scale format with the 40 faculty members and 7 librarians interviewed. From this we developed the final 30 statements.

Throughout the interview procedure all the faculty members proved very cooperative and many of them expressed considerable interest in the

TABLE 6.1
Field Test Responses to Item 13

	No Response	AAA	AA	A	U	D	DD	DDD
Number	2	9	29	51	19	69	36	19
Percent	.9	3.8	12.4	21.8	8.1	29.5	15.4	8.1

"The size of the library collection in my discipline should serve as a measure of how well the library will serve the needs of my students."

research. Most spoke freely and at some length in response to most of the questions. Nevertheless, we received the strong impression that many of them obviously had not specifically thought about library materials for undergraduates. They often responded only in the briefest manner to these questions. They could not describe how undergraduate library materials might differ from those needed for graduate students and researchers. Some listed specific library items from their disciplines. Others provided statements too general or too vague for use in the attitude scale. Many of their statements proved unclear, confusing, and meaningless both to other faculty members we interviewed and to the judges.

The faculty members interviewed seemed unable to describe at any length the characteristics of materials they selected for undergraduates. We found this curious for a group of highly educated and normally quite articulate individuals. We concluded that most faculty members do not have well-defined attitudes about the types of materials that are appropriate for undergraduates. Only one attitude statement related to library collections remained after the reviews and the pilot test. Item 13 stated, "The size of the library collection in my discipline should serve as a measure of how well the library will serve the needs of my students." This statement referred to the most obvious feature of library collections—size.

For attitude-scale construction, it is a good statement. The responses correlated (.22) at a statistically significant level (.01) with the total responses to all the other attitude statements (with it removed). Therefore, we concluded it measured an attitude part of the larger set of attitudes depicted by the scale—that is, library educational attitudes. In addition, faculty members usually responded either negatively or positively to this attitude statement (see Table 6.1).

Furthermore, through factor analysis, attitude statement 13 loaded strongly (.50) with the factor three statements. These statements described traditional attitudes toward the library. Faculty members associated with this dimension believed (a) the library is easy for undergraduates to learn how to use; (b) the library should be quiet; (c) enrollment of highly capable students results in more student library use; (d) small classes results in more student library use; (e) surrounding students by books in the library positively influences the students, whether they use the books or not; and (f) the size of the library collection in the discipline measures how well the library serves undergraduates. The factor analysis results supported our other conclusions reached from the interview and review procedure. That is, faculty members do not have well-defined and widely held attitudes about undergraduate library materials.

We spent almost 50 hours interviewing experienced undergraduate faculty members, dozens of hours writing and revising attitudes statements, additional hours getting reviews from qualified judges, and uncounted hours surveying 300 faculty members through two surveys at seven different colleges and universities. After all this effort, only one attitude statement about the nature of undergraduate library collections remained on the scale. This astounded us, and we looked for reasons.

We surmised that the study's methodology could have been faulty. Interviewees' responses always partially depend on the interviewer. The interviewer must instill confidence and secure insightful answers. The faculty members, however, did speak at length about other elements of the library's educational role. This allowed us to add several statements about these elements to the final attitude scale. Rejecting methological issues as a problem, we delved into issues related to attitude formation.

Attitude theory told us that individuals learn attitudes. If individuals have little or no contact with a particular phenomenon, then it is futile to ask them about their attitudes about it. They have not learned an attitude or have ill-defined attitudes towards the phenomenon. For example, it is probably pointless to ask natives of the inner jungles of New Guinea to express an attitude towards American basketball. If they have never seen the game played, they will not have an attitude towards it.

Anthropological linguistics provided us with further insights into the inability of faculty to articulate clearly a description of undergraduate library materials. Whorf (1956) observed that the Hopi Indians have one noun that describes every thing or being that flies, except birds. On the other hand, Eskimos use several words to describe snow. Hopi Indians can, of course, distinguish between, for example, insects and airplanes. They, however, have little reason to do so. Eskimos, on the other hand, have many reasons to make comparisons about the conditions of snow. For them, such comparisons may be a matter of life and death.

Anthropological linguists also have found in many languages a negative correlation between the length of a word or phrase and the frequency of its use. For example, Eskimos have learned through considerable comparisons to use only one word that adequately describes to other Eskimos a particular condition of snow. We can compare this with the several words or phrases that an English-speaking American television weather reporter uses to describe particular conditions of snow. Again, the differences reveal the relative importance of snow in each culture (Brown, 1958). We concluded for several reasons that the terms "undergraduate book" or "undergraduate journal" mean little to most undergraduate faculty members.

A REVIEW OF BOOK SELECTION FOR UNDERGRADUATES

Despite the difficulty of describing materials appropriate for undergraduate libraries, librarians need a clear and broadly applicable definition. Each year libraries buy hundreds of thousands, perhaps millions, of books for undergraduates. Since World War II, several large universities even have set up separate libraries specifically for undergraduates. For these libraries, the universities often bought additional copies or took books from the existing collections. How did they decide which books to add to these libraries? We thought an examination of their efforts might provide a definition of undergraduate materials.

Braden (1970) provided a review of several undergraduate libraries set up at large universities. Her investigations revealed that faculty members and librarians working together had little success in defining those books appropriate for undergraduates. For Harvard's Lamont Library, she found, "Probable use by Harvard undergraduates was the criteria for selection, rather than any theory of what would constitute an ideal book collection" (p. 15). At the University of Michigan, she reported, "No great effort was made to draw a sharp line between the graduate book and the undergraduate book" (p. 46). Librarians selected a title for the University of South Carolina Undergraduate Library if a faculty member had reasonable grounds for believing undergraduates would use it (Braden, 1970).

Several years before the opening of the Cornell University's Uris Library, planners tried to define the types of books appropriate for this undergraduate library. They concluded:

> It might be a book that a member of the faculty considers an undergraduate book, i.e., one put on a reading list. It might be a book that will or should be used two or three or four times a year. An undergraduate book would also be a book placed on reserve for an undergraduate course. It might be a "best book" or a standard title that every undergraduate should be exposed to. It might also be a book that would be an "invitation to learning" for students. (Braden, 1970, p. 101)

Often, from these efforts, institutions defined an undergraduate library book as a book that a faculty member thought should be in an undergraduate library.

This definition, of course, begs the question. It provided us with little insight as to why faculty members thought a book should be in an undergraduate library. How did a faculty member determine the placement of a book on a reading list or on reserve for undergraduates to use? Are the criteria for such selections the same or similar for all faculty members?

We next looked at efforts to define core collections. Even *Books for College Libraries* provided little help in defining undergraduate library books. In the preface of the first edition, the authors merely stated:

> *Books for College Libraries* is a list of monographs designed to support a college teaching program that depends heavily upon the library, and to supply the necessary materials for term papers and suggested and independent outside readings. It contains some information on all fields of knowledge, including areas not in a college curriculum. Within the limits of the allocation, each area contains some scholarly monographs for the use of faculty and exceptional undergraduate students. The collection is expected to satisfy independent curiosity (and recreational interests) of students and faculty. (Voigt & Treyz, 1967, p. v)

The preface to the second edition of *Books for College Libraries* quoted from the proposal for its compilation and publication. According to the proposal, this edition included:

> the bare minimum of titles needed to support an average college instruction program of good quality . . . without the support of large academic libraries or special collections [and] containing some information on all fields of knowledge of interest to the academic community. (ACRL, 1975, p. vii)

None of this gave us the definition of an undergraduate book.

The recent third edition of *Books for College Libraries* provided an elaborate description of the procedures used for the book selection. "Contributors were asked to keep in mind an imaginary college or small university that concentrates on the customary liberal arts and sciences curriculum but also offers work at the undergraduate level in business, computer science, engineering, and the health sciences" (ACRL, 1988, p. viii). The compilers, however, attempted no definition of undergraduate books. However useful and commendable their efforts, we suspect that other groups of reviewers would develop different lists. Throughout our review of the several lists of recommended books for undergraduates we did not find an acceptable definition of "undergraduate library materials."

RELATED STUDIES

Psychology Journals

We tried to determine if an operational definition of undergraduate materials existed. That is, do faculty members at different but similar institutions select the same library materials for their undergraduates? Do their students use similar library materials at each institution?

We examined the use of psychology journals at a liberal arts college and a research university (Hardesty & Oltmanns, 1989). Specifically, we compared the journals cited over a seven-year period by psychology honor students in the senior theses at Indiana University and DePauw University. We hypothesized that Indiana University students would cite more and different journals than the DePauw University students. The Indiana University students, after all, had ready access to a research library with over 200 journals directly related to psychology. The DePauw University students had ready access only to the libraries of a small liberal arts college with about 50 psychology journals.

We found, however, a statistically insignificant difference between the two group in the average number of citations. The Indiana students averaged citing 8.9 journal titles and 14.0 journal articles. Together, they cited a total of 38 journals three or more times. The DePauw students averaged citing 7.3 journal titles and 13.6 journal articles. Together, they cited 42 journals three or more times. At both institutions relatively few journals accounted for most of the citations. Twenty journals accounted for 80 percent of the DePauw University citations; 19 journals accounted for 80 percent of the Indiana University citations.

Did the students cite the same journals? Indiana students cited 19 journals not cited by DePauw students. DePauw students cited 21 journals not cited by Indiana students. In fact, the DePauw University libraries owned 8 journals not cited by it own students, but cited by Indiana students.

Did we discover a core collection of psychology journals for undergraduates? Even among the top 10 journals cited at each institution we found only modest overlap. We discovered 6 of DePauw's top 10 also in Indiana's top 10 list. Conversely, we found 6 of Indiana's top 10 in DePauw top 10 list. After a handful of heavily cited journals in common, each group of students largely went separate paths. We found little agreement based on use on undergraduate psychology journals. This finding conformed to findings of other studies. For example, Hogan and Hedgepeth (1983) found a few journals of general agreement and wide diversity following the small nucleus list.

The ACM Periodical Bank

The Associated Colleges for the Midwest (ACM) provided perhaps for undergraduate libraries the most noteworthy attempt to find an undergraduate journal collection. In 1968, 10 members of this consortium created the ACM Periodical Bank to reduce periodical costs through resource-sharing. According to Blair Stewart (1975), president of the ACM during the period, they founded the Periodical Bank under the following assumptions:

> The member colleges of ACM are relatively small liberal arts colleges with similar curricula and presumably, very similar needs for library services. It was assumed that these needs included in each library current subscriptions and backfiles for a basic core of something like 500 periodicals. (p. 371)

Stewart, however, soon discovered that the members' periodicals holdings were not "pretty much alike." Nor did he find a basic list of 500 title that all the libraries should have.

Instead, he uncovered only 73 periodicals to which all 10 of the libraries subscribed to in 1971. Investigating further, Stewart found member libraries uniquely held well over half of the 3,553 active titles. Most libraries held only 450 titles in common. He concluded librarians should not view these titles as a "basic list" that every liberal arts college should subscribe.

Furthermore, Stewart reported, during the three years studied, no one ever requested 2,795 periodicals, or 68.1 percent of the titles owned by the Periodical Bank. One library owned 2,037 periodicals not requested by any other library in three academic years. Stewart raised serious questions about the value of many of the periodicals when no one ever requested such a large number. He proposed that the number of libraries holding a title a useful, if indirect, sign of its probable value in a liberal arts college library. Clarke (1980) concluded from the Periodical Bank's experiences, "Little use was made of most periodicals held by college libraries" (p. 504).

Mathematics Journals in Selected Liberal Arts Colleges

We replicated the ACM study with a more limited focus (Hardesty & Hastreiter, 1988). In our study we concentrated on the periodicals of one discipline. We asked if periodicals holdings of only one discipline differed among similar institutions? Could we determine undergraduate journals within one discipline?

We identified the mathematics journals acquired by six colleges: Berea College, Davidson College, DePauw University, Eckerd College, University of the South, and Washington and Lee University. These institutions enroll between about 1,000 and 2,300 undergraduates. Each institution has a strong adherence to the liberal arts. From an examination of their college catalogs, we determined no significant differences existed among the six institutions in either number or type of mathematics courses offered.

We found, however, considerable differences among the institutions according to mathematics journals acquired by their libraries. The number of journals acquired ranged from 13 to 41 with costs ranging (in 1985) from $287 to $4,701. Purchase of the 66 mathematics journals and memberships held collectively among these six institutions costs over $7,100. Nevertheless, all six have in common only two mathematics journals, *American Mathematical Monthly* and *Mathematics Magazine*, which together cost slightly more than $80. The two mathematics journals represented only three percent of the 66 active mathematics periodicals subscribed to by the six institutions. This percentage is similar to the findings of the ACM study, which revealed that the 10 members libraries held in common two percent (73) of all the periodicals titles (3,553) to which they collectively subscribed. Is this the core mathematics journals on which all the mathematics faculty at the six colleges could agree? Most of the colleges held in common only 13 of the 66 periodicals. These 13 journals cost about $2,600.

We hypothesized that a relationship existed between the number and cost of mathematics periodicals and several variables (see Table 6.2). We first examined variables directly related to mathematics. These variables included the number of mathematics majors graduating in 1985 and the number of mathematics faculty members. We next looked at measures of library expenditures, including the periodical budget and the total library budget. Finally we considered total institutional measures, including enrollment, general and educational expenditures, total number of faculty, and endowment.

We found *no* positive relationships between the number and cost of mathematics journals *and* the number of mathematics faculty or graduates. We found *no* positive relationships between the number and costs of mathematics journals *and* the library budget and the periodical budget. Finally, we found *no* positive relationships between the number and costs of mathematics journals *and* general and educational expenditures, endowment, enrollment, or total faculty. In fact, we found the number and costs of the mathematics periodicals *inversely* related to the general wealth (endowment) of the institution and enrollment (see Table 6.3).

TABLE 6.2
Ranking of Variables

	Berea	Davidson	DePauw	Eckerd	Univ. of the South	Washington and Lee
Math. Graduates	10 (3)	20 (1.5)	20 (1.5)	5 (6)	7 (4)	6 (5)
Math. Faculty	7.4 (4)	7.5 (2)	10.6 (1)	4 (6)	9 (6)	7 (5)
Math. Journals	13 (6)	24 (4)	17 (5)	41 (1)	27 (2)	26 (4)
Math. Journals Costs	$287 (6)	4,068 (2)	1,045 (5)	4,701 (1)	4,052 (3)	3,978 (4)
Library Budget	$563 (5)	734 (3)	579 (4)	295 (6)	807 (2)	932 (1)
General & Educational Expenditures	$11.5 (5)	13.5 (3)	18.1 (1)	10.4 (6)	12.7 (4)	17.5 (2)
Endowment	$131.8 (1)	38.1 (5)	50.0 (2)	4.8 (6)	47.2 (3)	45.2 (4)
Enrollment	1,550 (2)	1,390 (3)	2,331 (1)	1,040 (6)	1,100 (5)	1,271 (4)

Note. Rank in parenthesis.
Note. Mathematics periodical costs included professional society memberships; library and periodical budget in thousands of dollars; endowment and general and educational expenditures in millions of dollars.
Note. Library budget and enrollment information are from *American Library Directory*, 37th ed., 1984, New York: R. R. Bowker. Copyright © 1984 by R. R. Bowker. Reprinted by permission.
Note. General and educational expenditure and endowment information are from *1982–1983 Voluntary Support for Education*. New York: Council for Financial Aid to Education, 1984.

TABLE 6.3
Spearman Rank-order Correlations

	Number of Mathematics Journals	Cost of Mathematics Journals
Mathematics Graduates	−.75*	−.41
Mathematics Faculty	−.42	−.37
Library Budget	.08	−.08
Periodical Budget	.48	.48
General and Educational Expenditures	−.37	−.37
Endowment	−.77*	−.94*
Enrollment	−.94*	−.77*
Total Faculty	−.67	−.75*

*Significant at .05 level

FACULTY CULTURE AND UNDERGRADUATE LIBRARY MATERIALS

While well-versed and articulate about the complexities and subtleties of the subject matter of their respective disciplines, we found faculty members often strangely tongue-tied in discussions of the selection of undergraduate library materials. It seemed as if we had asked the natives of New Guinea to define American basketball. When we looked for agreement about undergraduate library collections and their use, we found diversity. Similar institutions held different journals. In fact, the same discipline at comparable institutions sought different journals. Undergraduates with the same assignment at dissimilar institutions used different library materials. How could we explain this?

Lack of Preparation for Undergraduate Teaching

Farber's "university-library syndrome" provides an important perspective into the faculty's inarticulate responses. Faculty members, concluded Farber (1974a), "view the college library's relationship to their teaching much as they viewed their university library's relationship to their graduate studies" (p. 14). Graduate education trains faculty members to analyze critically books, journal articles, and related items. They learn how to judge these materials by their accuracy, relevance to the advancement of knowledge, and similar criteria. Nevertheless, faculty members have received little formal education on how to select library materials for undergraduates. Nor have their graduate experiences prepared them for how to encourage undergraduates to use these materials. Nevertheless, many members of the faculty remain fully confident in their library skills. Whatever skills they had they learned largely without the guidance of a librarian. Following the mythology of their culture, most faculty members believed such help unnecessary.

We found this explanation compatible with other aspects of faculty culture. Gaff (1975) noted the widespread inability of faculty members to express clearly their teaching goals. He quoted one instructional developer who lamented, "Many faculty members with whom I work do not even know what they are trying to do" (p. 52). Graduate education has not prepared faculty members to deal with many aspects of undergraduate education.

Specialization and Individualization

In many ways we found faculty culture discouraged the development and use of undergraduate libraries. It rewards individuals for focusing on one small aspect of a discipline or subdiscipline. Faculty members frequently devote their lives to something that appears to outsiders as quite esoteric. The books and journals in their areas also may appear esoteric to outsiders, such as undergraduates. Many faculty members, however, because of their biased perspective, selected these materials for the undergraduate library. Yet, their education did not prepare them to stimulate student use of these materials.

The same faculty culture that encourages specialization also encourages deference to that specialization. Academic freedom has come to include many prerogatives in the classroom. Some faculty members would expand these prerogatives to include the selection of all the library materials in their area. To many, who else could do it better? As one economist asked us (in response to our showing him *Books for College Libraries*), "Why is that list any better than something I would draw up?" To him, it was not. He had spent years drawing up his list through the book order slips submitted annually to the library. A check of his institution's library economics holdings, however, revealed little overlap between it and *Books for College Libraries*. To this faculty member that was so much the worse for *Books for College Libraries*. Studies of large differences among collections of some not-so-imaginary small colleges and universities should not surprise us.

Nonuse of Library Materials

We conclude that the diversity among undergraduate libraries reflected the dissimilar interests of the professors who guide the undergraduates. The specialized interests of faculty members often result in them directing undergraduates into narrow research areas. This, of course, perhaps fosters a much needed and healthy intellectual curiosity among the undergraduates. It also increases the difficulty for the librarians to predict and to support the undergraduate needs. Finally, this emphasis on narrow specialties may even frustrate the undergraduates and encourage their disenchantment with the library.

We found considerable nonuse of library materials in our several studies of undergraduate libraries (Hardesty, 1981a, 1981b, 1988a, 1988b; Hardesty & Hastreiter, 1988; Hardesty & Oltmanns, 1989). Undergraduates often quite successfully undercut the most determined faculty's efforts to involve students in the academic world. In particular, Becker, Geer, and Hughes (1968) determined from their study of college grades, "A substantial number of students apparently had no use for books that would not be helpful in attempting to meet requirements" (p. 98).

Frequently, the advice of faculty members and the recommendations from *Books for College Libraries* and *Choice* have little influence on the reading selections of undergraduates (Saunders, 1982). Schmitt and Saunders (1983) found that about one-fourth of the 188 titles favorably reviewed through *Choice* for undergraduate libraries remained uncirculated after two-and-a-half to three years in the Purdue University libraries. Almost half (44 percent) of all the books placed on reserve at DePauw University during one semester received no use (Hardesty, 1981b). Perhaps these unused materials represented unsuccessful efforts by faculty members to convince students that highly specialized library materials met goals of undergraduates. Librarians may predict incorrectly the direction of scholarly curiosity. Faculty members overestimate it.

Acquisition of Library Materials Not to be Read

Faculty members recommend the purchase of library materials for other reasons than use by undergraduates. As we noted earlier, faculty members seek library materials to support their specialized teaching and research. Conceivably, however, faculty members seek the acquisition of library materials with no thought of their actual use.

Support of Learned Societies.

In our study of mathematics journals we found often that use had little relationship to decisions about the starting or dropping a particular publication subscription. One mathematician wrote us:

> Some periodicals are publication of professional societies, and their purchase serves to support these societies. Faculty members and students may be members of these societies, but do not necessarily *read* the journals [Emphasis added]. (Hardesty & Hastreiter, 1988, p. 8)

Richard DeGennaro (1977) in his classic article wrote:

> some of the learned societies have come to view their publishing operations
> as a means of generating income from library subscriptions in order to subsi-
> dize low-cost members' subscriptions and other desirable activities rather
> than simply as a means of disseminating the scholarly knowledge of their
> field. (p. 70)

Learned societies may need additional support. Nevertheless, most library
directors, faced with increased demands on a finite budget, have little enthusiasm to commit the library's budget for such purposes.

Psychological Value.

Another variable, not fully appreciated by librarians, explains the acquisition of unused library materials. DeGennaro touched upon this variable in
citing the economists William J. Baumol and Junusz A. Ordover. They
wrote:

> The fact is that a growing proportion of scientific journals have virtually no
> individual subscribers, but are sold almost exclusively to libraries, and that a
> very high proportion of these journals are rarely, if ever, requested by read-
> ers. This suggests that many journals provide services primarily not to readers
> but to authors for whom publication brings *professional certification, career ad-
> vancement,* and *personal gratification* [emphasis added]. (cited in DeGennaro,
> 1977, p. 69)

This variable is the psychological value of unused opportunities. People
attach a significant value to the existence of certain opportunities whether
they use them or not.

Davis (1974) provided an example of this phenomenon in giving reasons people like living in the New York City area. An investigation found:

> The responses typically included a substantial listing of cultural facilities such
> as museums, art galleries, and theaters. Yet the people who listed these fac-
> tors did not, in general, use them—they did not go to the theater, art galler-
> ies, or museums. The value of the cultural facilities was not related to actual
> use. Having them there in case they ever did want to go appeared to be the
> significant value. (p. 75)

We can add libraries and the materials they contain to the list of inadequately used resources that provide psychological value to individuals.

Faculty members often propose the purchase of library materials for its
"psychological value." They give little thought to use. They may claim
need for the materials to support institutional or departmental accredita-

tion. Perhaps accreditation agencies should examine the use of materials they require. Another rationale for such materials is "to attract new faculty." Will these new faculty use the materials? Faculty members also may defend library materials on the basis that "every *good* institution should have it" or "we need it to be respectable." Are these rationales based on predictions of *actual use* or *psychological need*? We suspect the latter.

CONCLUSIONS

Therefore, despite faculty members considerable association with both libraries and undergraduates, we conclude that most seldom think about the types of materials needed for undergraduates. Questions about materials for undergraduate libraries did not conjure up a richness of well-developed and shared attitudes among the faculty members we studied. Even using many words and sentences, individuals could not describe their attitudes clearly. We determined that faculty members seldom made or discussed such comparisons among their colleagues.

We do recognize often that a wide variance exists both among and within books. They vary according to format, readability, scope of interest, and other characteristics. Even the most experienced individual may find difficulty in discriminating among the different purposes for which a single book might be appropriate. From our review of core lists for undergraduate libraries, we cannot say that librarians either have developed a widely accepted definition of undergraduate library materials.

Almost 40 years ago, distinguished librarian Louis Round Wilson wrote, "Although colleges spend a considerable proportion of their educational budgets for library materials and services, the contribution that the libraries make to further the educational program is less than it should be" (Wilson et al., 1951, p. 13). Wilson called for a closer cooperation among administrators, faculty, students, and librarians for the development and use of the library. He wanted the library, in his words, "created *by* as well as *for* all the college community" [emphasis his] (p. 13).

Wilson et al. (1951) saw that many faculty members had inadequate preparation for the responsibilities of selecting library materials and of stimulating their use by undergraduates. Neither in their school and college experiences nor in their graduate education had faculty members received thorough instruction in the use of library materials. Almost two generations later, Wilson's observations remain accurate.

The norms of faculty culture make it difficult for faculty members to improve their teaching through learning from their colleagues (Gaff, 1975). Through a tradition of academic freedom, faculty members have come to believe that a professor's classroom is his or her castle. They believe, "It is somehow unprofessional for a faculty member to criticize, interfere with, intrude upon, or even observe another instructor in his classroom" (Gaff, 1975, p. 3). These cultural norms also impede discussion and coordination among faculty members in their selection of library materials for undergraduates. As a result, as Lyle (1974) noted, "The selection of books is haphazard and incomplete, and in many cases, even with the best instructors, likely to be superficial" (p. 178).

We propose from our study that faculty culture frequently sanctions the purchase of little-used library materials. Even for faculty members at small liberal arts institutions, the model of the research university remained strong. Faculty culture holds that teaching competency comes with subject expertise. Faculty culture also holds that this same specialization qualifies one to select materials for the undergraduate library. To question this prerogative is to question ones' credentials and to threaten academic freedom. Few subjects arise more sensitivity among faculty members.

In their deference to the research model, many faculty members seek the development of large libraries and the acquisition of specialized materials in their area. Frequently, they give inadequate thought to the use of these materials. The psychological need for library materials is no less *real* or deeply felt than the need for library materials that undergraduates will use. Versatile displays by librarians of cost and use data will not easily sweep aside psychological issues of status, prestige, and personal gratification. These matters often explain why many faculty members choose to work in academia in the first place.

chapter seven

FACULTY CULTURE: A HISTORICAL PERSPECTIVE

INTRODUCTION

During the past century or so the faculty has developed a distinct culture. While librarians are part of academia, they seldom either share or fully appreciate the values of the faculty. Most librarians have quite different academic credentials than do most faculty members. Librarians enter the profession with a master's degree in library science. While increasingly a two-year degree, the socialization period for a master's degree in library science is both shorter and less intense than for most faculty members. It requires neither in-depth research nor specialization. The education of librarians emphasizes the application of knowledge.

On the other hand, most prospective employers require the Ph.D., a research degree to enter the faculty. Potential members of the faculty receive this degree only after an intensive and extensive period of study and socialization. Graduate study *requires* prospective faculty members to specialize. In fact, this dedication to specialization is the most distinguishable characteristic of faculty culture. From this commitment, other faculty values originate. Faculty culture values autonomy, research and publication ideals, and the pursuit of knowledge for its own sake. These values often manifest themselves when faculty members emphasize the transmission of knowledge or defend prerogatives in the classroom.

Faculty members, of course, share these commitments in varying degrees. Several researchers caution us there is no such animal as the "faculty member." Certainly, within any group, whether it be doctors, lawyers, automobile workers, or librarians, we do violence to the individual when we concentrate on the multitude. Generalizations about the faculty are particularly risky because of the diversity of its members. Nevertheless, we can lose any useful grasp of faculty culture if we look only at the individual. To comprehend faculty attitudes toward the library's role in undergraduate education we must understand faculty culture.

Within this chapter we only touch upon the prominent attributes of faculty culture. There is a growing richness of information about the faculty, and we refer the reader to several major works. The following is only representative and not inclusive of this literature. Notable histories include Rudolph's *The American College and University* (1962), Veysey's *The Emergence of the American University* (1965), and Brubacher and Rudy's *Higher Education in Transition* (1968). Rudolph's *Curriculum: A History of the American Undergraduate Course of Study Since 1636* (1977) provides the most extensive history of undergraduate education.

The earliest extensive study of the faculty is Wilson's classic *The Academic Man* (1942), updated two generations later as *American Academics Then and Now* (1979). Caplow and McGee's *The Academic Marketplace* (1958) reported on the impact of academics' newly found job mobility in the 1950s. During the 1960s Jencks and Riesman published their time-honored study on the development of faculty culture, *The Academic Revolution* (1968). The 1970s saw published Ladd and Lipset's excellent work on the politics of faculty, *The Divided Academy* (1975a).

The 1980s has witnessed a proliferation of literature on higher education. Reflecting both changes in society and higher education, much of this literature is highly critical. Major works include: Bowen and Schuster's *American Professors: A National Resource Imperiled* (1986), Boyer's *College: The Undergraduate Experience in America* (1987), and Clark's *The Academic Life* (1987). While successful in stimulating current discussions, these works have not yet passed the test of time to take a place along with earlier classics.

Several authors have published useful and readable literature reviews. They include Shulman's *Old Expectations, New Realities: The Academic Profession Revisited* (1979), Austin and Gamson's *Academic Workplace: New Demands, Heightened Tensions* (1984), Finkelstein's *The American Academic Profession* (1984), and Kuh and Whitt's *Invisible Tapestry: Culture in American Colleges and Universities* (1988). In providing a background to and in discussing the current situation, we refer to other major works that the reader may want to examine.

HISTORICAL DEVELOPMENT

Early History

Some recent critics of higher education have looked back almost nostalgically at the early days of higher education in this country. For example, Clark (1987) wrote:

Faculty members were still relatively homogeneous. They shared some common knowledge, were thrown together in a common didactic cause, and, typically, were proficient in Greek and Latin. Indeed, in the seventeenth and eighteenth centuries, educated people could be interested simultaneously in mathematics, the sciences, literature, philosophy, music, and the fine arts. (p. 27)

Perhaps, these critics gained some comfort from an age when all agreed on the measure of an educated person. Close examination of this time, however, reveals an arrangement unacceptable to most faculty members today.

Early higher education had a strong vocational purpose—the training of ministers. Towards that purpose, the colleges followed a traditional course of study set up in the European universities by the middle of the 13th century. The liberal arts, as put forth by the ancient Greeks, included a strong measure of rhetoric, logic, grammar, arithmetic, geometry, astronomy, and music. The first three subjects (the *trivium*) consisted basically of a study of Latin (Rudolph, 1977). Early colleges offered only a few courses—all compulsory. For example, the nine students of Harvard's first graduating class took courses centered around the classical languages and literature and the Bible. The president taught all the courses during the three-year curriculum (Carnegie Foundation, 1977).

Later, tutors helped the president. Most of these young men had just received their degrees, and they served while awaiting a ministry. Despite their inexperience by standards of today, they taught all subjects. In fact, a single tutor had the responsibility for both the intellectual and spiritual development of a single class throughout its four years (Finkelstein, 1984). Enforcement of chapel attendance, disciplinary regulations, and daily recitations prevented close relations between the tutors and the students (Brubacher & Rudy, 1968). These early tutors had little job security, nor did they seek any. Since most would soon enter the ministry, they viewed teaching as only a temporary career.

While the tutors taught everything, they did not necessarily teach any one thing well (Rudolph, 1977). They used recitation as the primary teaching method. Students repeated from memory, often word for word, the textbook assignments. Latin served as the language of instruction and discourse, and Greek and Hebrew also played important roles in the instruction. Students spent hours executing "almost deliberately uninviting exercises in Greek and Latin grammar and mathematics" (Veysey, 1973).

By the late 18th century a few changes started taking place. In 1767, Harvard tutors begin to specialize by teaching only one subject to all classes

(Rudolph, 1977). Few colleges, however, followed this early lead. Philanthropic bequests, again first at Harvard, made possible professors to begin to supplement the tutors. With this small core of permanent faculty, college teaching began as a lifelong career. As had the tutors before them, these new professors came from the higher socioeconomic sector of society (Finkelstein, 1984).

The early 19th century saw both a growth in existing institutions and in new institutions. Yale faculty doubled between 1800 and 1820. The Brown and Harvard faculty grew by 50 percent (Finkelstein, 1984). The stimuli of religious influences and the "community building" of the period resulted in an a "college movement" (Rudolph, 1962). Increased competition among religions and newly found job insecurity among ministers led to the beginning of many colleges (Finkelstein, 1984). Most of the founders had not gone beyond the classical courses of undergraduate studies of the older institutions of Harvard, Yale, and Brown. Outside of Harvard, few faculty members had postbaccalaureate training in their teaching specialty (Finkelstein, 1984).

They seldom had any specialization nor any interest in specialization. Some presidents, in fact, interpreted attempts by faculty members to specialize as disloyalty to the institution. In their opposition to specialization, the presidents had considerable support among the egalitarian ideals of early 19th-century society. Wrote Higham (1979):

> To parcel out segments of work or knowledge, so that the responsibility of each person contracts while his dependence on others increases, violated the American ideal of the untrammeled individual and its corollary, the jack-of-all-trades. Moreover the intellectual specialist affronted egalitarian values; he dealt in secrets only a few could share. (p. 4)

The president might ask the professor who taught the sciences also to take on sophomore Greek for a year. The classics professor might spell the president in his moral and political philosophy course while the president preached or raised funds (Schmidt, 1957). Few regarded college teaching as requiring advanced knowledge or specialized study (Bowen & Schuster, 1986).

Rudolph (1977) concluded that during the period that most of the colleges edged towards superficiality. Sloan (1971), however, provided a more favorable view of higher education of the early 19th century. He held that the ideals of higher education of the period look very much like the ideals of recent reformers. He noted the emphasis on teaching and concern with the quality of student life. The colleges stressed personality development, community experience, and consideration for the moral ends and social purposes of knowledge.

Rudolph (1977) concluded that colleges of the pre-Civil War sought to avoid confrontation with several ~~inherit~~ truths:

inherent

> A college course can contain everything a student needs to know, college authorities know best what that is, a student's special aptitudes and interests are a poor guide to what he should study, the mind is a set of muscles with inherent faculties that can be trained only by a demanding course in ancient languages and mathematics. (p. 84)

Critics of these colleges considered them ineffective institutions. Nevertheless, throughout the period the colleges remained committed to a prescribed classical curriculum and controlled by the churches (Sloan, 1971).

The *Yale Faculty Report of 1828* epitomized the philosophy of the pre-Civil War colleges. In this report, President Day strongly defended the order of the day, such as daily recitations and the use of a single textbook. Many historians of higher education believe this report set back reform for another 50 years. Sloan (1971), however, concluded the report, "did not differ in any of its essentials from the views held by most of America's foremost champions of university reform at the time" (p. 243). The "old-time college" had as its main purpose undergraduate preparation for later more self-directed professional and graduate studies. With limited resources, the college needed to resist trying to offer something for everybody. The college had to take its parental and supervisory responsibilities seriously because of the age (14 to 18) of most of its students (Sloan, 1971).

Far from conflicting with society, the antebellum college paralleled society. During the early part of the 19th century, professors gradually replaced amateur scientists and scholars (Shils, 1979). By the 1820s most important scientists held academic positions. In fact, demand exceeded supply. In many of the small colleges one professor would frequently teach all the courses in the sciences (Sloan, 1971). This expansion did not, as some have claimed, "break apart the classical curriculum" of the time (Finkelstein, 1984).

Before the Civil War, religion and science served in harmony at most colleges. Sloan (1971) wrote:

> As a rising, young professional group, scientists sought to avoid conflict with the theologians, the older, established keepers of the culture, and to draw some of the cultural prestige of the theological profession to themselves. . . . Scientists themselves sincerely believed in the religious dimensions of their subject and were eager to make them known. (pp. 236–237)

Scientists lived within a culture dominated by the religious issues of the day. Revival preaching and student conversions became standard features of college life. Both presidents and faculty encouraged, led, and controlled college revivals. According to Sloan (1971):

> Revivalists founded colleges teaching science and the classics; scientists sought the experience of sublimity in their research and evidences of divine harmony in natural law; and classicists lent their support and participation to natural history societies and technological institutes. (p. 227)

Gradually, however, changes did occur during this period. Between 1828 and 1860 the total number of science professors increased tenfold (Guralnick, cited in Clark, 1987). Science began to move beyond the realm of the amateur and the generalist. The fixed curriculum strained to cope with the secularization and the diversification brought by the sciences. Gradually, European-educated professors replaced the generalists. In 1850, President Wayland at Brown University increased offerings in applied science and technology and introduced the elective principle (Sloan, 1977). These reforms foretold the sweeping changes in higher education to come after the Civil War.

The First Academic Revolution, 1865 to 1918

By the mid-1850s the old system showed signs of breaking down. By then nearly one-quarter of the Brown University faculty took leaves for European study. Two of them had returned with European Ph.D.s. As faculty members gained mobility, institutional commitments weakened (Finkelstein, 1984). Change did not accelerate, however, until after the Civil War. Harvard expanded the curriculum in 1869 when it enlarged its elective system. The newly formed land-grant colleges furthered the broadening of the curriculum far beyond the classics. The founding of Johns Hopkins University in 1876 transplanted to this side of the Atlantic German graduate study. Eventually the Ph.D. became the mark of American faculty members.

Specialization.
The Ph.D. did not immediately take over. As late as 1884, Harvard had only 19 professors with the Ph.D. degree. Michigan had only six Ph.D.s on its faculty of 88 (Rudolph, 1962). Several factors slowed the adoption of the German model. The German university drew upon a rigorous academic high school known as the *Gymnasen* (Rudolph, 1977). The lack of a strong high school system forced many American colleges to operate preparatory schools. In fact, frequently the entire college curriculum barely operated above this level. This hardly offered a place for the highly trained specialist (Carnegie Foundation, 1977). In addition, the German university certified

entrants in the civil service and controlled entry into the elite professions (Rudolph, 1977). The egalitarian American tradition offered no such ready market for the colleges. The explosion of knowledge during the latter half of the 19th century, however, provided a fertile ground for elements of the German system.

In their emphasis on major examinations, the German system allowed more laxity in the daily operations. Often lecture series and terms varied. The Americans, however, altered the German system to their own needs. They responded to the excessive moralism of the earlier period with an insistence on objective, verifiable knowledge (Jencks & Riesman, 1968). They set up a more impersonal and bureaucratic education (Veysey, 1973). The Americans downplayed the broad education of the German degree and emphasized its research aspect. Within a democracy, the Ph.D. offered a standard entrance requirement to an academic specialty (Higham, 1979).

By the turn of the century, the Ph.D. had become the mark of respectability for all departments (Knapp, 1962). Professors formed learned societies and started journals. They began to identify with a particular academic discipline. Their service to it through publications, committee work, and meetings often conflicted with institutional needs (Knapp, 1962). The attachment to disciplinary communities extending beyond the individual institution received support from yet another source.

The presidents, trustees, and faculties competed for more Ph.D.s as a matter of personal reputation (Shils, 1979). The rivalry among colleges and universities led them to further the spread of the research model (Grant & Riesman, 1978). Gradually, the university gained ascendancy over other institutions of higher education. Even faculties of undergraduate colleges came to be staffed by scholars trained as researchers. As the Ph.D. spread, it changed the nature of higher education.

In 1903, William James (1903) called the Ph.D. an octopus. As it reached out to every reputable college, he questioned whether it assured effective teaching. He disapproved of Harvard's raising of standards for the degree in competition with other universities. In particular, he feared the results of the excessive organization (Rudolph, 1962). Once set up, the organization required research. Research and specialization, while leading to exciting advanced knowledge, also led to departmentalization (Rudolph, 1962).

Departmentalization.
Higher education began to take on the characteristics with which we identify it today. Institutions moved toward secularization and faculties rid themselves of their executive and judicial duties (Brubacher & Rudy, 1968). With the increase of scientific and technical knowledge and the elective system, the classical curriculum and emphasis on the training of

clergy diminished. Increasingly, faculty members reduced their responsibilities for character developments (Knapp, 1962).

As enough subject specialists converged, faculties organized themselves into departments. At first departments served as an efficient way to group faculties and the areas of knowledge they studied. Later they served as ways to divide the money and facilities of the university (Levine & Weingart, 1973). Soon, however, these faculties transferred strong allegiances to their departments (Hawkins, 1979). The departments also served as the faculties base for power (Riesman, 1980). The department served as a society of equals. With the Ph.D., each faculty member could specialize with a maximum degree of independence. Each could have his or her own sphere of influence. Faculty members charted career paths through the department as they set up new ranks from instructor to full professor (Finkelstein, 1984).

Unlike the German system, every Ph.D. in the American system could aspire some day to become a full professor. Therefore, the department did not center around one individual. Prospective faculty members had a systematic program controlled by the department through which they could enter academia (Parsons & Platt, 1975). Junior faculty members had clear steps to follow to the professorship. The department provided a way to accommodate the specialist. While specialization isolated faculty members, the department held them together (Hawkins, 1979). The balance of power among faculty, trustees, and presidents changed as departments increased in influence (Higham, 1979).

Professionalism.

In the pre-Civil War colleges, the faculty seldom challenged the president's power. They had little security and tenure did not exist. Wrote Schmidt (1957), "the professors were more like day laborers than professional people" (p. 95). The pre-Civil War professor served as *assistants* to the president (Shils, 1979). After the Civil War, however, increased specialization encouraged professionalization of college teaching. Who could challenge the professor in his own small segment of knowledge? With specialization, the faculty member would no long serve as an interchangeable part.

The professors sought primacy in determining the nature of their own work (Clark, 1987). By the early 20th century the faculty members claimed unquestioned authority within the classroom. Concepts of academic freedom and tenure soon developed as tensions grew between higher education and religious and secular powers. Around the turn of the century several faculty members became involved in causes that tested this concept. The faculty members held they had the right to explore and expound ideas contrary to the desire of their institution or society (Rudolph, 1977). In 1915 the General Declaration of Principles of the American Association of University Professors declared university teaching "no more subject to the control of trustees, than are judges subject to the control of the President" (Hofstadter & Smith, 1961, p. 866). The life of learning became a calling.

Control of the Curriculum.

With the increased specialization and professionalization of the faculty came increased control of the curriculum. The old classical curriculum had lost its authority. By the late 19th century, college faculties had developed an authority that made "the course of study a jealously guarded compound of special interests" (Rudolph, 1977, p. 18). The elective system soon evolved into the idea of a major field of study. As early as 1885 President Jordan of Indiana University had developed the idea of a major field of study. Only the increased specialization and expansion of knowledge would allow an area of interest and concentration in which a student moved from basic to advanced work (Rudolph, 1977). By 1910 most colleges and universities had adopted the subject major (Rudolph, 1977). With the major came other elements of modern higher education: the unit system for credit, the numbered course, the lecture, and the seminar (Veysey, 1973).

De-emphasis on Undergraduates.

The increased number of specialists expanded the course offerings. As faculty members became interested in an area, eventually it made its way into the curriculum. The curriculum became a vehicle through which faculty could pursue their areas of interest. Rudolph (1977) reported:

> In 1870 at Harvard 32 professors taught 73 courses; by 1910 the professors numbered 169, the courses 401. Somewhere between those professors and the courses in 1910 were twice as many instructors of less than professorial rank. The curriculum of 1910 in theory allowed a student to do what he wanted to, but it did not show him how and it put great distances between him and the senior professors. (p. 206)

In their pursuit of knowledge, the new professors often overlooked the undergraduates. Some new universities, such as Clark, Johns Hopkins, and Chicago tried to leave them out almost entirely (Riesman, Gusfield, & Gamson, 1971). The universities, however, found they could not do without undergraduates.

While they did not completely forsake the undergraduates, faculty culture came to value more highly graduate education than undergraduate education. Research and publication became more important than teaching, advanced courses more important than introductory courses, teaching of nonmajors less important than teaching of majors (Gaff, 1983).

During the 1880s and 1890s major institutions allowed faculty members to leave behind temporarily their teaching responsibilities through paid leaves of absences and sabbaticals. The faculty responded, as expected, with further research and writing (Rudolph, 1962). To those faculty members who did not produce research, some institutions began to respond by telling them to go elsewhere (Rudolph, 1962).

Changes in Teaching.

As emphasis on undergraduates waned, new teaching methods entered the curriculum. The lecture replaced recitation. With the increase in knowledge, recitation became less satisfactory as a way to convey needed information. Attempts to transplant the graduate seminar to undergraduate discussion groups proved expensive and difficult (Rudolph, 1977). Several curricular devises accompanied the lecture, including use of the library. Rudolph (1977) reported that about 1880 Harvard undergraduates began using the library in significant numbers to prepare research papers for their seminars.

Reserved reading shelves, theses, reports, and source books all involved the library. Other methods included laboratory work in sciences and field work (Rudolph, 1977). During this time institutions expanded both their libraries and laboratories. How much they expanded to benefit the undergraduates or the faculty members is another question. Frequently libraries grew as the new research professors demanded both the purchase of library materials and the publication of their own work. In 1900, Frederick Jackson Turner demanded as a condition for his willingness to stay at the University of Wisconsin, "enlargement of staff, fellowships, *permanent funds for the purchase of books*, a leave of absence, and *provisions for publications of historical studies*" [emphasis added] (quoted by Rudolph, 1977, p. 409).

Consolidation.

The period ended with the consolidation of several of the changes. The formation of the Association of American University Professors institutionalized concepts of tenure and academic freedom. The National Conference Committee and American Council on Education defined the American college. Unlike the 1828 Yale Report, they did not try to define the nature of the training and the subjects appropriate for a college education. Their definition acknowledged the importance of the department and strengthened the subject matter specialist. Faculty members had to have completed at least two years of graduate school. The institution must have a record of achievement in preparing its students for graduate school. It distinguished between preparatory school work and college work. Finally it required a library of at least 8,000 volumes, exclusive of public documents (Rudolph, 1977). The changes that occurred in higher education between the Civil War and World War I set up the base for present-day faculty culture.

Incorporation of Change, 1918 to 1945

The decades between World War I and the end of World War II continued the evolution of faculty culture. While the post-World War II surge in higher education eclipsed earlier growth, higher education expanded dramatically during the 1920s. Between 1910 and 1930 student enrollments increased from 266,654 to 924,275 and the number of faculty members from 33,631 to 71,722. Graduate education grew even more rapidly than undergraduate education. In 1910, 9,370 students enrolled in graduate schools, which awarded 409 Ph.D. degrees. In 1930, 47,255 students enrolled in graduate schools. The number of Ph.D. degrees awarded escalated to 2,024 (Link, 1955). Historian Arthur Link (1955) wrote of this period, "College and university faculties enjoyed greater respect and freedom than ever before in American history" (p. 332).

In their enthusiasm for the university movement, some highly respected leaders of higher education prophesied the disappearance of many colleges. They forecast the reduction of other colleges to the status of academies or junior colleges (Rudolph, 1962). The ideals of the college, however, never completely surrendered to the university movement. The movement for liberal culture gained strength at Harvard when Lowell succeeded Eliot as president in 1909 (Hawkins, 1979). By World War I, most colleges had successfully set four years as the time to receive an undergraduate degree (Jencks & Riesman, 1968). During the 1920s and 1930s the opponents of the university movement even mounted a counter movement to the proclivity towards specialization. Bennington, Sarah Lawrence, the University of Wisconsin, and the University of Minnesota, for example, tried to revitalize some of the values of the old curriculum.

Many of the faculty members of the post-World War II era have a certain nostalgia for this period. Jencks and Riesman (1968) wrote, "There is a myth that college freshmen used to know three languages, wrote limpid prose with flawless spelling and punctuation, and had a thorough knowledge of history and literature" (p. 511). They, however, found that an analysis of College Board examinations and freshman courses quickly dispelled this image as fantasy.

The better liberal arts colleges continued to incorporate university values into their own. As they proceeded to add research scholars to their faculty, these professors, in turn, sought to include more like-minded colleagues on the faculty. Together, they tried to change the liberal arts curriculum into professional specialties. More and more faculty members came to view the undergraduate liberal arts curriculum as preparation for graduate work (Jencks & Riesman, 1968).

In 1942 Logan Wilson published his classic work *The Academic Man.* Even with the depression, the number of Ph.D. degrees granted annually had continually increased. By 1939, 90 institutions awarded 3,088 doctorates (Wilson, 1942). Leading universities and liberal arts colleges had firmly instituted faculty culture much as we now know it. Despite developments since before the turn of the century, Wilson remained concerned with the status of American professors. He asked, "One may wonder why in this country the academician commands respect but not great amount of popular envy" (Wilson, 1942, p. 148). He answered that America had never made a place for an aristocracy of intellect. The diverse social composition of the academic profession prevented a high degree of class consciousness. Nevertheless, Wilson's work showed a high degree of concern with status and prestige. Fully two-thirds of his book dealt with these issues.

External Careers.
During this period, another change occurred. Faculty members started to have external careers, particularly with government. The spread of higher education and the identification of faculty members with scholarship provided America with a larger reservoir of specialists than that of any European country (Oleson & Voss, 1979). As the role of government expanded, it needed specialists and turned to the professors.

While Governor of New York, Franklin Roosevelt began to consult faculty members and even to appoint them to various state administrative posts. When he became president, Roosevelt formed the core of his "brain trust" with Columbia University faculty members (Ekirch, 1969). Only a few individuals, such as Walter Lippman, expressed concern about the mix of the pursuit of knowledge and the exercise of political power (Ekirch, 1969).

World War II provided additional conditions for faculty members to serve the federal government. With loyalties to the local institution already weakened by disciplinary ties, service to the government provided yet another channel for faculty specialization. In addition, the armed forces depleted the supply of college-age males. Higher education turned to the government for rescue. Many a G.I. spent part of the duration on a college campus in a military training program. By the end of the war contracts with the army and navy accounted for as much as 50 percent of the income of some men's colleges (Brubacher & Rudy, 1968). At the time, few would predict accurately the deluge of servicemen who would later converge on the campuses. Few also would foretell the dramatically increased role of the federal government in higher education after the war.

The Second Academic Revolution, 1945–

Higher Education For Everyone.
The surge in higher education after World War II completely overshadowed its previous growth. In 1870 about 50,000 students enrolled in insti-

tutions of higher education (Rudolph, 1962). By 1930 enrollment had increased to slightly more than a million. With the depression and the War, enrollment remained at about that level in 1944. Once the War ended, however, veterans returned in droves to take advantage of the educational opportunities offered by the Servicemen's Readjustment Act of 1944, more popularly known as the G. I. Bill of Rights.

At the time, this legislation did not represent a national commitment to the principle of federal aid for all deserving college students (Brubacher & Rudy, 1968). Through this legislation the government sought to ease the transition of members of the armed forces into civilian employment. An early estimate concluded that only about 10 percent of those eligible would take advantage of the opportunities presented. Within four years, however, higher education enrollment increased to more than double the 1944 level (2,403,000) (Bureau of Census, 1975).

By 1956 (the year before Sputnik), enrollment had increased to 2,918,000, which represented 19.5 percent of the population 18 to 24 years old. By the time the first "baby boomers" began to enroll in college (1964), the figures had climbed to 4,950,000. This represented 26.3 percent of the 18- to 24-year olds (Bureau of Census, 1975). Before enrollment peaked 20 years later, it reached almost 12.5 million students (Bureau of Census, 1987).

What happened to the faculty? At the turn of the century the 24,000 faculty members represented only .08 of one percent of the labor force (Lipset & Ladd, 1985). By 1944, faculty had increased to about 150,000. Within eight years (1956) faculty doubled to almost 300,000. By 1964 they reached almost half a million (Bureau of Census, 1975). By the early 1980s they had reached over 850,000 (Bureau of Census, 1987).

From where did they come? At the turn of the century, American institutions awarded annually only about 400 doctorates. By 1940 this had increased to slightly more than 3,000. By 1950 the number of doctorates awarded had more than doubled (6,600). The next 20 years saw it surge even more. By 1970 the doctorates awarded annually reached almost 30,000 (Bureau of Census, 1975). In the mid-1970s it approached 35,000 annually before stabilizing (Bureau of Census, 1987). For almost 40 years higher education has continually expanded and offered a ready employer for most of the tens of thousands of newly awarded Ph.D.s.

Expansion of the Federal Government's Role.

In late 1947 and early 1948 the President's Commission on Higher Education for Democracy issued its six-volume report under the general title *Higher Education for American Democracy*. This report held that Americans should be able to carry their education as far as their capacities permitted. The authors proposed a system of community colleges and federal college scholarships. It also proposed federal aid to help the severely strained college and university facilities (Zook, cited in Brubacher & Rudy, 1968). Resisted by some, including President Hutchins (1948) of the University of Chicago, this report foretold massive federal intercession in higher education.

At first the federal government granted funds to those attending institutions rather than to the institutions themselves. The government had set a precedent for this policy during the 1930s when it supported individual students through the National Youth Administration. While technically the G.I. Bill payments went to the individual student, the institutions of higher education benefited. Brubacher and Rudy (1968) described a series of federal programs from the G. I. Bill to the Surplus Property Act of 1944 to federal research grants that supported higher education immediately after World War II. In 1947 alone some two-and-half billion federal dollars went to higher education.

The 1950s saw passage of the National Defense Act of 1958 the year after the launching of Sputnik. From 1956 to 1960 federal aid to higher education more than doubled. In 1965 Congress passed the Higher Education Act, and the next year federal support tripled the 1960 level (Bureau of Census, 1975). By then the federal government had become a major benefactor of America's higher education.

Even by the early 1960s researchers began to notice the impact of various forms of federal aid on higher education. A Brookings Institution study in 1962 found:

> The Government (and vaster historical forces) has divided the liberal arts faculty into a contingent of relatively young scientists and social scientists with lighter teaching loads, higher incomes, substantial research support, and other prerequisites, and another contingent of older humanists, with heavier teaching loads, lower incomes, and little research support. (Orlans, cited by Brubacher and Rudy, 1968, p. 237)

Federal funds support research far beyond any support before World War II. Together with the surge in enrollments after the War, federal funds helped to build what Riesman (1980) has described as "the pyramid of graduate study and research that characterizes today's American universities, as exemplified by virtually all the members of the Association of American Universities" (p. 43).

Impact on Faculty Culture.

The post-World War II expansion and infusion of federal funds have further shaped faculty culture. Those faculty members who entered the profession between 1958 and 1968 experienced a decade of continual growth in both enrollments and federal funding. While the base for the modern faculty culture existed well before World War II, the events after the War solidified it. Faculty benefited enormously from this growth.

An academic career gained status equivalent to other professions as more and more of society perceived higher education as supporting important social goals (Shulman, 1979). Research became even more of an ideal. Research chairs became common at the top of the academic system (Veysey, 1973). Caplow and McGee (1958) showed that by the 1950s research and publication often became the sole criteria for employment and advancement. Demand for faculty members remained high, and this demand, which increased mobility, allowed faculty members to achieve satisfying careers. They gained more voice in both their own selection and evaluation and in administration. Prestige, important social goals, and job mobility became major attributes of the academic culture (Shulman, 1979).

Those faculty members who entered academia during the so-called "golden years" often became highly socialized by their early experiences. They passed their values and expectations on to those who came later. Some have suggested that these years have taken on a mythology undeserved. Henry (1975) commented:

> The term "affluence" is a misnomer as a description of the period. It is an error to apply the concept even in the sixties. The cost per student calculated upon costs for basic operations did not increase significantly beyond the normal rate of inflation. The notion that money for higher education was easy to get or that funds were available for the asking is an illusion; such an idea rests upon invalid comparisons and short memories. (p. 150)

Some have suggested neglecting basic institutional needs and mortgaging the future financed the "golden years" (Carnegie Foundation, 1977). Others have suggested that the post-Sputnik period, like the 1890s, was something of a quirk (Veysey, 1973). They contend that the bulk of the changes made between 1958 and 1968 represented little more than tinkering with innovations first introduced during the 1920s. Nevertheless, the changes made during this time became an integral part of the ideal faculty culture (Shulman, 1979).

Retrenchment in Higher Education.
Quirk or not, faculty members regard the gains made from the late 1950s to the late 1960s as an integral part of an ideal faculty culture (Shulman, 1979). However, beginning about 1968, it became clear that costs began to exceed income prospects. Colleges and universities began to suffer from declines in enrollments. By the early 1970s academia recognized a declining job market in many areas. Many predicted a grim future for higher education (Shulman, 1979).

For faculty members, the past decade-and-a-half has been a period of uneasiness and bewilderment. During the period of growth, increased centralization of academic governance reduced the faculty's role in academic governance. Even the funds from the federal government did not come without complications as the federal government increased its insight into academic affairs. The financial difficulties of the 1970s and 1980s further reduced the options of the faculty. It is no wonder that faculty have perceived in recent years a loss of professional autonomy (Shulman, 1979).

Freedman et al. (1979) concluded that much of the confusion and bewilderment is because of unfulfilled faculty expectations. They noted:

> Particularly in the years after World War II professional development has taken place along a single dimension. Socialization in graduate school has been a matter of producing a physicist, a chemist, a sociologist, an authority in English or French literature. One's status in the field—obtaining the Ph.D., attaining tenure at a major university, earning promotions—depends upon one's ability to push out the frontiers of knowledge in one's discipline another notch or two. (p. 4)

Upward career mobility became determined by one's disciplinary orientation. Those faculty who entered academia after World War II entered a culture offering prestige, recognition, and mobility all based on an emphasis of research first and teaching second. During the 1960s, the faculty at the most prestigious institutions gained the independence that served as the model for the rest of the academic profession.

Higher education, however, did not maintain the sustained growth for the rest of the profession to realize this model. In fact, the large cohort that entered the profession in the 1960s has created a "bulge" of tenured faculty members. Unfortunately, these faculty members severely limit job opportunities both for new faculty members and for themselves (Altbach, 1985). Concluded Shulman, "For most academics, higher education no longer promises the excitement of prestigious careers, rapid advancement, and professional prerogatives that it did through the 1960's" (p. 4). Instead, a career in higher education offers considerable uncertainty.

SUMMARY

We state the obvious, of course, in declaring that contemporary faculty culture is the product of its historical development. Nevertheless, we can understand contemporary faculty culture only in the context of its historical development. Without looking backward, it is difficult to comprehend and appreciate its current situation.

The specialization that began to occur before the turn of the century led to both a sense of mastery and professionalism among the faculty. Faculty members came to believe that only they have the understanding to control the curriculum and even to govern themselves. Increased specialization, however, also reduced the common elements among the faculty. It promoted departmentalization and reduced institutional loyalties. It de-emphasized the education of undergraduates.

The post-World War II period further changed faculty culture. While providing funds for higher education, the federal government policies emphasized research and external career opportunities over teaching of undergraduates. As enrollments grew, administrators assumed an increasingly important role in institutional governance. In times of growth and ample career opportunities, the increased role of administrators and conditions attached to federal support may have seemed unimportant to faculty. More recently, however, the current retrenchment in higher education has reduced career opportunities. More and more, faculty members perceive administrators, the federal government, and others as encroaching on their prerogatives. As we leave the 1980s and enter the 1990s, faculty culture is full of uncertainty and apprehension.

chapter eight

CONTEMPORARY FACULTY CULTURE

INTRODUCTION

Understanding contemporary faculty culture is of no small importance. Bowen and Schuster (1986) underlined significance of faculty culture in *American Professors: A National Resource Imperiled* when they wrote:

> The nation's faculties are entrusted with the education of about a third to a half of every cohort of young people, and they touch the lives of millions of other persons in less intensive encounters. They train virtually the entire leadership of society in the professions, government, business, and to a lesser extent, the arts. Especially, they train the teachers, clergy, journalists, physicians, and others whose main function is the informing, shaping, and guiding of human development. (p. 3)

The faculties, concluded Bowen and Schuster (1986), are "a major influence on the destiny of the nation" (pp. 3–4).

Understanding the faculties, however, also is no small undertaking. Clark (1987) has pointed out the necessity of considering the "sheer scale of American higher education" (p. 54) to help the understanding of contemporary faculty culture. Some 3,000 institutions, enrolling almost 12 million students, employ 700,000 to 800,000 part-time and full-time faculty members (Clark, 1987).

The divergence among the faculty almost prevents identification of a common culture. There may be a longing for a sense of community among the faculty. Nevertheless, according to Boyer (1987), they live and work within disciplines and institutions with sharply contrasting values and practice. Within the profession there are basically dissimilar sets of responsibilities. Unlike most cultures, faculty culture encourages a high degree of individuality among its members. Clark (1987) noted that faculty culture values originality in research, flair in teaching, and creativity in personal interpretation. The well-known nature of faculty members to intellectualize ideas to extinction thwarts conformity and consensus. Some observers, however, such as Bowen and Schuster (1986), contend that a faculty culture does exist and that we can treat the faculty as a closely knit social group with certain common values.

VALUES

Sources of Values

Graduate study plays a dominate role in the transmission of the academic tradition to the new generation of faculty. This socialization occurs more readily than at first apparent. Graduate study is both an extensive and intensive experience which occurs during an important formulative period of an individual. Most faculty members share the experience of advanced study at only 100 to 150 leading graduate institutions in this country (Bowen & Schuster, 1986). This limits the diversity of the experience.

No doubt some members of the faculty may have eluded or resisted the socialization of the graduate experience. They, however, meet further socialization efforts in their first academic positions (Bowen & Schuster, 1986). They will find even an institution of lesser prestige emulating the values and attitudes of the more prestigious graduate institutions (Bowen & Schuster, 1986). Indeed, faculty members of community colleges often share many of the values of the faculty members of four-year institutions (Bowen & Schuster, 1986).

Across all types of institutions, faculty members share a strong belief in education. Through education, faculty members often see themselves as "actively engaged in providing man's best hope for improvement" (Clark, 1987, p. 222). Some will assert passionately, "Secular learning is a sacred calling." A calling binds self-interest to a larger common good. Critics, however, contend that some faculty members use such convictions to sanction self-indulgence (Eble, 1983).

The process through which faculty members enter the profession influences their attitudes and values. Most drifted into it out of love for research and knowledge acquisition. Eckert and Stecklein's (1961) study of Minnesota faculty found that almost half of those interviewed never had really aspired to be college teachers. The faculty members found themselves in the field largely as a result of what seemed to be chance happening. The process of become faculty members seldom seems to fit a purposeful design (Eble, 1972).

Graduate education emphasizes research and knowledge acquisition and largely attracts those interested in these areas. Only indirectly does it prepare faculty for teaching. Indeed, Bess (1982a) concluded that many faculty members by nature do not enjoy the social interaction central to teaching. The result is often a faculty poorly suited and prepared for the role of undergraduate teacher. Bowen and Schuster (1986), strong supporters of the professorate, concluded:

> The faculty in place during the 1980s is generally considered to be highly capable in terms of intelligence, energy, advanced degrees, and mastery of their special fields. Yet, in the opinion of many thoughtful observers, they have serious shortcomings: their education has been highly specialized and lacks the breadth that would be desirable for the mentors of undergraduate students; they identify more fully with their disciplines than with their institutions, and many of them are more highly motivated for research than for pedagogy; their teaching style fails to take advantage of innovative teaching methods of proven efficacy. (p. 282)

Once committed to the profession, faculty members face teaching tasks about which they know little or nothing. They frequently find the tasks difficult and frustrating to perform (Bess, 1982a). This situation gives an underlying source of tension and stress in faculty culture.

Jencks and Riesman (1968) concluded that those colleges that believe in general education will never grow in numbers or influence unless or until they can socialize prospective faculty members in less than a complete academic culture. These colleges need faculty members with more emphasis on the relationships of knowledge and inquiry and less emphasis on coverage and depth within a single discipline. These colleges need faculty members with graduate training that reflects the undergraduate teaching expected of the faculty. Unfortunately, most young faculty members, in getting their doctorates from major research institutions, imitate their own professors and make only minimal adaptations when they go out to teach undergraduates (Riesman et al., 1971).

The Increase of Knowledge and Specialization

Many specialized fields now exist that did not exist even a generation ago. At the graduate level this may have occurred because of the "knowledge explosion." Nevertheless, we must wonder about the necessity of this fragmentation of knowledge as fields constantly divide and subdivide. Specialization has resulted in course proliferation on a "grand scale" (Veysey, 1973). Wrote Barzun (1968), "Every specialist wants his own course; all are specialists from an early age; the sum of these specialties swell the number of courses" (p. 192). At the undergraduate level, the expansion of knowledge may provide less of a rationale for this course proliferation.

More likely, colleges add courses as a result of the attraction towards the mastery of a narrow subject area. Even at the undergraduate level, young faculty members have a strong need to establish themselves. They can do this by emphasizing teaching and research in their specialties (Levine, 1978). Faculty members may feel compelled to teach a few courses considered essential to the instructional goals of their department. As part of the bargain, however, they seek to add courses that allow them to practice their specialized skills (Mayhew, 1962). To guarantee adequate enrollments, often faculty members must form coalitions involving requirements for majors and graduation (Carnegie Foundation, 1978).

Martin found that 85 percent of the faculty respondents in his "Standard Bearer" institutions regarded teaching in the area of specialization as very important. He concluded faculties at the liberal arts colleges, lacking alternative models, will press their institutions toward measures of success used by the research universities "as fast as the school's resources and their own persuasiveness permit" (Martin, 1968, p. 229).

There, of course, are several pitfalls to this course. Few departments can hire specialists in all subfields. Therefore, a college department may lean heavily towards one philosophical orientation or subspecialty rather than have a broad perspective (Carnegie Foundation, 1978). The curriculum may lack any internal logic and consistency (Mayhew & Ford, 1971). As a result, undergraduates may end up with fragmented and limited knowledge (Study Group, 1984). Authors of a recent study concluded, "As for what passes as a college curriculum almost anything goes" (Project on Redefining, 1985, p. 2).

Many argue for such specialization based on graduate school requirements. Most undergraduates, however, do not enter graduate school or even enter careers related to their undergraduate majors. Therefore, specialization may poorly serve them (Mayhew & Ford, 1971). One critic noted that because of the emphasis on the accumulation of knowledge in narrow areas "we face the tragic reality that we have not turned out students who even grasp the significance of the catalogue statements of educational goals, let alone incorporate them into their lives" (Cross, 1975, p. 61).

This emphasis on specialization and on the accumulation of knowledge also creates stress among the faculty. Bowen and Schuster (1986) noted, "All competent faculty members live with the sense that they are dealing with infinity—that they can never fully catch up" (p. 69). Bayer (1973) found that almost one-third of the faculty agreed with the statement "knowledge in my field in expanding so fast that I have fallen seriously behind" (p. 15). Barzun (1968) commented, "The teacher-scholar is hampered by the shortness of the twenty-four-hour day and his inability to be in two places at once" (p. 53). Considerable stress also arises from the differences between the relative importance institutions and faculty give to teaching, research, and service (Seldin, 1987).

Critics also contend that increased specialization has eroded the sense of collegiality and community among colleges (Astin, 1985). Eble (1972) found that schools concerned with teaching undergraduates have more collegiality among the faculty. As faculty members first identify with their discipline, they feel less institutional loyalty. Clark (1987) referred to the "tribes of professionals" (p. 257). They develop strange patterns as they seek to isolate and command a domain of work (Clark, 1987). The strong identification with specialties and subspecialties has resulted at many research universities, noted Astin (1985), in a "social environment . . . characterized by parochialism, jealousy, and denigration of the work of others" (p. 187).

Faculty members de-emphasize other aspects of learning beyond the accumulation of knowledge in the specialties. Wrote William Stephenson (1980), professor of biology at Earlham College:

> All librarians know that college faculty persons are disciplinary chauvinists. We faculty don't want to give up the time our students spend on subject matter for training in literature accessing skills. We don't want to learn from librarians. We feel that the most effective learning is learning in our narrow subject matter disciplines. I don't want to give up time in biology for "less important things." (p. 81)

Often a faculty member closely limits students' learning to the professor's narrow subject area. Undergraduates seldom fully develop the skills needed for lifelong learning in the liberal arts tradition.

Whatever the merits of specialization, the accompanying increase in knowledge has created problems in undergraduate education. No longer can planners satisfy queries about the curriculum by how much of the world's knowledge undergraduates should try to acquire. "Such questions are unanswerable" (Carnegie Foundation, 1977, p. 119), wrote the authors of the Carnegie report *Missions of the College Curriculum*. They argued:

> Measured against all that is now collectively known by human beings, the ignorance of even the wisest and most educated person grows every day. So does the stock of knowledge to be sampled, and the challenge to colleges to convey it to their students effectively.
>
> The most obvious consequence of the growth of knowledge for the curriculum is that in any four-year period, the proportion of the world's total knowledge a college can offer to its students inevitably will be less than that of the period that immediately preceded it. Moreover, it is becoming harder for colleges to insist that any specific amount and kind of knowledge is adequately representative of everything that there is to know. (p. 40)

Some argue that for scientific progress to occur that academics must have the opportunities and incentives to work in specialized fields (Blau,

1973). Others argue that faculty members must cultivate other constituency other than their own students if they are to avoid becoming captives to them (Riesman et al., 1971). Certainly, because of the present reward structure in higher education, many young professors have little difficulty in concluding that the rewards go to specialists.

Professionalism

In academia, Eble (1983) noted, "The individual's urge to be a professional, which implies being a specialist—physicist, historian, cosmetologist—is overpoweringly strong" (p. 84). Faculty, however, are unlike other professionals, who depend on client approval for financial support. Faculty members are independent of virtually all evaluation except peer review (Shulman, 1979). In addition, faculty members are uniquely dependent upon an organizational setting to meet their career goals (Shulman, 1979). Finally, in contrast to other professionals, faculty members vary considerably in their knowledge and responsibilities (Austin & Gamson, 1984). These characteristics result in a unique set of professional prerogatives.

A most important professional prerogative for faculty members today is a high degree of autonomy. Eckert and Stecklein (1961) found this to be one of the major satisfactions of the faculty members they interviewed. Faculty members claim that they alone can set the standard of specialized competence and judge the performance of individuals (Blau, 1973). In fact, some faculty members believe that faculty alone can decide even the direction of the institution (Hefferlin, 1971).

Faculty members, however, have more influence than power. Their influence comes from their status as professionals based on specialization rather than position in the hierarchy. Therefore, in matters such as finance where their knowledge is less, faculty members have less influence (Austin & Gamson, 1984).

Under the rubric of "academic freedom" faculty have expanded claims of professional prerogatives to the exercise of numerous rights. For example, academic freedom has long meant the right to espouse unpopular ideas. Wrote Caplow and McGee (1958) in their major work *The Academic Marketplace*, academic freedom assumes:

> that men working on the fringes of established knowledge will often dissent from the truths of the majority, will appear unreasonable, eccentric, or disloyal, or will be unable to explain to others their motives for pursing a particular line of effort. (p. 222)

The needs of scholarship and scholarly creativity are somehow special. Academic freedom has come to mean a tolerance for error, a respect for the unknown, a need for inquiry and continued proof, and a spirit of suspended judgment (Rudolph, 1962).

Some of the rights are peculiar to the profession. Academic freedom also has come to mean that faculty members have the right to teach in privacy (Levine & Weingart, 1973). This includes the prerogative to plan the sequence, content, and methodology of instruction. It includes the right to decide how to evaluate students. Faculty members even may view visits to the classroom by department chairpersons and colleagues as unwarranted intrusions (Carnegie Foundation, 1977).

Faculty prerogatives can make change very slow. Hefferlin (1971) quoted a professor who declared, "You can make all the rules and regulations you want, but if a professor of microbiology is always going to teach the way he's always taught, you're stuck" (p. 15). Because of the sanctity of the classroom, faculty members frequently do not even know of teaching innovations by their colleagues (Wilson, Gaff, Dienst, Wood, & Bavry, 1975).

Professional prerogatives entail authority over the curriculum. This includes the composition of courses for a major, the requirements for a degree, and the determination of suitable depth and breadth for a liberal education (Blackburn, Armstrong, Conrad, Didham, & McKune, 1976). In arranging and rearranging individual courses, faculty curricular committees, however, "do not touch upon the ways in which professors organize their materials, teach their classes, and examine their students" (Bok, 1986, p. 71).

The faculty members have a limited perspective. According to the authors of a major work on the college curriculum:

> Members of curriculum development groups know something about their own experiences as students, professors, or administrators; but these experiences rarely include formal exposure to the knowledge and experiences of others. Most college faculty members, despite their Ph.D.'s, often have not experienced more than one form of curriculum, read a single book on educational philosophy or learning theory, or even heard that over two hundred other colleges already do what they think they are inventing. (Chickering, Halliburton, Bergquist, & Lindquist, 1977, p. 121)

Concentration, reported Rudolph (1977), is the style known and approved by most faculty members. Therefore, studies reveal a persistent tendency towards increased specialization and more electives in the major—at the expense of general education (Levine & Weingart, 1973).

When it becomes the "will of the faculty" to change the curriculum, the most likely result is more specialization in the form of senior projects, senior theses, reading courses, independent study, honor programs, and more demanding term papers (Rudolph, 1977). The avoidance of debates on kinds of inquiry and discussions needed to improve learning, according to Bok (1986), "probably constitutes one of the reasons why our colleges have not managed to help their students make more impressive gains in such important areas as the capacity to think rigorously or to write with clarity and style" (p. 71).

Knowledge-oriented faculty members have other reasons for emphasizing specialization in the undergraduate curriculum. Curricula devised by specialists strengthens their authority. Clark (1987) found, "The more arcane the materials, the more powerful the claim to self-determination" (p. 185). A more general curricula may threaten the professional status and rewards of faculty members. Faculty members quickly form a maze of "distribution requirements" to protect their "narrow interests" (Clark, 1987, p. 185). In addition, few faculty members will admit that their subject is not essential to every educated person (Grant & Riesman, 1978).

Increasingly, faculty members have successfully sought involvement in the selection of top administrators (Jencks & Riesman, 1968). Administrative and professional considerations frequently conflict, particularly since administrators usually do not share many of the biases of the faculty (Blau, 1973). In curricular matters, administrators are more likely to focus on breadth, distribution, and general education (Rudolph, 1977). In many ways, the concerns of administrators more closely match those of students than those of the faculty (Mayhew & Ford, 1971). Therefore, faculty members have become increasingly active in assuring the selection of administrators who will not intrude on academic freedoms.

Faculty members also seek a voice in recruitment, appointment, promotion, and the tenure process of their peers. Selection of colleagues has become increasingly important as faculty members have organized into departments. Departments strengthen the power of specialists through their collective authority (Clark, 1987). Departments provide a bulwark against increased institutional bureaucracy and emphasize universalistic standards of performance and competence (Parsons & Platt, 1975).

Departments, however, can accentuate differences among the faculty. Every department, wrote Barzun (1968), wants more faculty, more space, more library purchases, more secretarial help, more research assistants, and more frequent leaves—while every other department must stay put. To those who can further their interests, departments provide jobs and promotions (Chickering et al., 1977). In addition, through their control of the major, they can severely restrict curriculum change (Rudolph, 1977). Boyer (1987), for example, found among colleges more "curriculum tinkering rather than genuine reform" because of an emphasis on "protecting departmental turf" (p. 87). In addition, Blau (1973) concluded that faculty appointment power often leads to poor selections.

Professionalism in academia also has resulted in a curious set of divided loyalties among faculty. Declared Barzun (1968):

And inside the house the scholars, who repeat that *they* [emphasis his] are the university, complain of the work and the pay like wage earners, while declaring that their allegiance is not to the particular place but to their subject specialization, their "discipline." (p. 6)

This orientation allows the faculty member to view his institution as "a temporary shelter where he can pursue his career as a member of the discipline" (Caplow & McGee, 1958).

"Paradoxically," concluded Blau (1973) from his major study on the academic work place:

The very qualities of faculty members that make them attractive colleagues and enhance commitments to the institution where they work make them less committed to the institution, and the qualities that raise a faculty member's own loyalty to his college or university reduce that of his colleague. . . . The source of the paradox is the academic prestige system. (p. 127)

Faculty members usually consider well-known scholars as respected colleagues. Therefore, researchers may attract increased allegiance of others to an institution. These scholars, however, are less dependent on and loyal to the local institution (Blau, 1973). They feel more responsible to peer review by members of their discipline at other institutions (Clark, 1987). Parsons and Platt (1975) noted that in a truly bureaucratic organization the outside loyalty to a discipline would be a conflict of interest.

Probably only a few colleges have such reputations that loyalty to discipline and institution merge (Caplow & McGee, 1958). Nevertheless, some researchers contend that as status increases, loyalty to the institution increases. Senior professors active in research, therefore, may have strong loyalty to both institution and discipline (Austin & Gamson, 1984).

On the other hand, faculty members who emphasize teaching usually have more limited academic reputations. This restricts their mobility, and they may feel more loyalty to the institution. These faculty members, however, are less desireable colleagues, and large numbers of them weakens loyalty to an institution (Blau, 1973). In addition, Blau (1973) concluded that many faculty members with only a local perspective seem to impede education innovation. Therefore, an institutional emphasis on teaching may reduce the value of an academic community in the eyes of most faculty members (Blau, 1973).

Academia does not uniformally distribute the rewards of professionalism. Clark (1987) noted, "Type of work goes a long way in academia in determining the extent and form of authority" (p. 184). Certainly there are advantages to teaching within ones specialty. Faculty members do not have to water down the insights and subtleties. They do not have to deal with large numbers of students, often uncommitted to the subject (Riesman et al., 1971).

Teaching outside the discipline in interdisciplinary majors "may require faculty members to devote enormous amounts of time" (Carnegie Foundation, 1977, p. 197). In addition, departments often consider nonmajor and interdisciplinary activities as undermining their influence. Therefore, junior faculty members interested in financial or professional advancement will seek to teach in their specialties (Levine & Weingart, 1973).

Despite the flaws of professionalism, Clark (1987) concluded, "In knowledge-driven organizations, where knowledge is the end as well as the means, a fragmented but intense professionalism is the only effective guarantor of standards" (p. 268). Faculty, not administrators or students, are the most ardent defender of the conventional standards of academia. The administration is too removed and too lacking knowledge of the subject to provide control. While tenure protects academic freedom and enhances professionalism of the faculty, it is the normative control of the faculty that insists on the highest professional standards of individual faculty members (Parsons & Platt, 1975).

Research and Publication

The literature on teaching and researching in higher education during the past 20 years reflects their importance to faculty members. Clark (1987) concluded the mix between these two primary responsibilities of faculty members is crucial in shaping the profession. Despite considerable investigation, the impact of both tasks on faculty members remains unsettled. Recent researchers have arrived at different conclusions. For example, Clark (1987) met among faculty members "remarkable little resentment about 'publish or perish' " (p. 84). Bowen and Schuster (1986), on the other hand, found "considerable tension . . . attributable in some measure to the heavy emphasis on research" (p. 147). What then do contemporary faculty members think about research and publication?

Graduate education strongly emphasizes research and publication. Graduate students quickly learn that publication brings rewards. In recent years, the socialization to research has become even stronger among faculty cohorts (Corcoran & Clark, 1984). "Most faculty," wrote Ladd (1979), "seem to believe that the most meritorious behavior of an academic man or woman is the performance of significant research" (p. 5). Even at the junior college level a large percentage of faculty members express some interest in doing research (Rich & Jolicoeur, 1978).

Trow and Fulton (1975) reported, "There is no question that publication sharply enhances an academic's chances of high salary, and also of earnings outside the university" (p. 75). The monetary returns, even for the first article, are often large (Tuckman, 1976). Research faculty also receive the rewards of higher prestige and status (Blau, 1973). A "publish and flourish" mechanism clearly operates in higher education (Trow & Fulton, 1975).

Clark (1987) found the rewards more than extrinsic. He concluded, "Research professors like to do research. They learn to do it in graduate school, if not before; they learn to like it on the job" (Clark, 1987, p. 84). Even after faculty members are no longer concerned with tenure and promotion they continue to publish (Áustin & Gamson, 1984).

A prominent faculty view is "no one can be a good teacher unless he does research" (Ladd, 1979, p. 6). Freedman et al. (1979) found a strong belief among faculty members that "the higher the level of competence they attain in a subject the more they can offer to students" (p. 93). Bowen and Schuster (1986) concluded that research "enlivens teaching" (p. 18).

Is there a conflict between research and teaching? Jencks and Riesman (1968) found no evidence that the two are antagonistic. Wilson (1979) also reported finding no conflict. Even Blau (1973), while concluding that good researching and teaching did not go hand in hand, concluded they are not incompatible. In fact, research time usually comes from faculty member's leisure and family activities rather than from teaching duties (Harry & Goldner, 1972). Wilson et al. (1975) found that most faculty members believe that research even improves teaching. What then is the problem?

The problem is that nearly all faculty members teach, but only a minority significantly engage in research. Thirty years ago, Caplow and McGee (1958) declared:

> For most members of the profession, the real strain in the academic role arises from the fact that they are, in essence, paid to do one job, whereas the worth of their services is evaluated on the basis of how well they do another. (p. 82)

In the 1970s, Ladd and Lipset (1975b, 1975c, 1976) revealed just how much faculty do publish. Ladd (1979) wrote:

> Nearly three-fifths of all those employed fulltime in professorial positions have never brought to publication any sort of book written or edited singularly or in collaboration with others. In all, just under one-fourth of American professors have published extensively. . . . Over half have published nothing or very little. (p. 3)

Other researchers have found similar results. Trow and Fulton (1975) reported that over half of faculty members surveyed had not published a single research or scholarly paper in the preceding two years. Willie and

Stecklein (1982) also found nearly half (49%) of their Minnesota faculty reported no books, monographs, or articles in the preceding two years. More recently, Bowen and Schuster (1986) reported that faculty members devote, on the average, not more than a fifth of their time to research.

Austin and Gamson (1984) concluded that faculty members often receive mixed signs as to how to parcel their energies. Many faculty members remain unclear about the roles expected of them (Rich & Jolicoeur, 1978). While their education trains them as researchers and a majority remain interested in research, Ladd (1979) concluded "most faculty [members] don't like research and don't do it very well" (p. 5). He found most faculty members prefer teaching and the daily demands of their jobs require them to concentrate on it (Ladd, 1979).

Institutional pressures may come into play. The National Enquiry into Scholarly Communications (1979) found an increase in publication in the 1970s because of academic unemployment and competition for advancement. Willie and Stecklein (1982) discovered that faculty members at four-year institutions published more than faculty members 20 years earlier. They, however, also found more recent faculty members spent less time on research and scholarly writing.

Few faculty members can avoid some stress related to research and publication. Most think they should be engaging in scholarly research. Eble (1983) noted, "Few can be found who will not speak of work in progress, perpetually and incompletely for most. And few, too, who do not compromise their actual teaching by this burden of being or appearing to be productive" (p. 72). Even those faculty members who do publish encounter some tension. Freedman et al. (1979) determined that faculty members at research-oriented institutions experience considerable stress from their own high aspirations. He noted, "No matter what their accomplishment, it is not likely to measure up to their expectations" (p. 93).

The problem, then, is the graduate school socialization of faculty towards research and publication. Only a small portion of the faculty at a few major universities, however, can devote most of the time to research and publication. Most faculty members experience personal preferences or organizational constraints that incline them toward teaching. They must work out an uneasy accommodation between their graduate school orientation and what they want to do. The domination of the research ideal, whatever its merits, makes for an anxious faculty.

Teaching—and the Library

Several investigators have asserted that the American academic system is primarily a teaching system (Trow & Fulton, 1975). Most faculty members spend most of their time teaching and most of them report a strong interest in teaching. For example, Boyer (1987) found that 63 percent of the faculty members in his study declared their interests "lie toward teaching as opposed to research" (p. 128). Rich and Jolicoeur (1978) reported that faculty members at all types of schools place considerable emphasis on teaching.

The system, however, is full of paradoxes and contradictions. However much faculty members like to teach, the conviction that research is its cornerstone has shaped academia (Boyer, 1987). Research, not teaching, receives the largest share of rewards. As Clark (1987) noted:

> Most professors teach most of the time, and large proportions of them teach all the time, but teaching is not the activity most rewarded by the academic profession nor most valued by the system at large. Trustees and administrators in one sector after another praise teaching and reward research. Professors themselves do the one and acclaim the other. (pp. 98–99)

The authors of *Integrity in the Colleges Curriculum* concluded, "Research, not teaching, pays off in enhanced reputation, respect of peers beyond one's own campus, and access to funds" (Project on Redefining, 1985, p. 10).

"With few exceptions, young professors know that, if they wish to gain tenure or an appointment at a highly rated institution, they will need to achieve distinction not by good teaching, but by an impressive record of research and publication," observed Boyer (1987, p. 125). A young professor we interviewed at a large research university confirmed this view. He remarked, "I am up for tenure next year. To get tenure I have to be a good researcher but only an adequate teacher. I don't have time to get to know the undergraduates." A more experience faculty member at another research institution flatly declared to us, "Teaching is tolerated, but not rewarded. The name of the game is research."

Still, many faculty members regard teaching as a major source of satisfaction in their lives (Wilson et al., 1975). They commit themselves to teaching. We interviewed many such faculty members. One faculty member even wrote library papers along with students to show them how to write as an example. Students perceive these faculty members as the most effective teachers (Eble, 1983). These faculty members also exhibit the most loyalty to the local institution (Eble, 1983). Their commitment to teaching and to the local institution, however, is at a price.

Faculty members highly committed to teaching often remain at institutions in the lower and middle levels of the academic hierarchy. They have the heaviest teaching loads with more than their share of average to below-average students (Clark, 1987). These faculty members usually have lower salaries and less mobility. Nevertheless, Boyer (1987) found these faculty members dedicated to teaching despite "eroding incomes and quality of campus life" (p. 138). Whatever institutions may want, concluded Austin and Gamson (1984), teaching-oriented faculty members emphasize teaching, and research-oriented faculty members emphasize research.

Graduate education, however, slights preparation for teaching. Its main emphasis is the command of the knowledge of a field and a demonstration of research competence (Eble, 1983). Frequently any introduction to teaching comes only incidentally or not at all (Project on Redefining, 1985). Katz (1962) noted:

> The teacher arrives in the classroom unprepared . . . not in his own knowledge, but for communication. The college teacher probably has never had even once the experience of systematically analyzing a single classroom hour in terms of the effectiveness of his job in communicating what he knows. (p. 371)

Cross (1975) concluded, "No graduate schools turn out faculty members prepared to think with sophistication about the teaching of undergraduates" (p. 63).

This is clearly true about teaching undergraduates how to use the library. Many of the faculty members we interviewed declared they had to learn on the job how to engage undergraduates in the academic library. Several reported it took a long time for them learn the job.

Others have never overcome the obstacles. They complained, "There is no reward for the extra effort needed to get students to use the library." "It is just not worth the hassle," recounted one. In fact, there are even some risks. Cautioned one faculty member, "Students do not appreciate the effort and may turn on the instructor."

Obviously the logistics can be burdensome. Several faculty members at large institutions mentioned departmental pressures to offer large classes which, they asserted, prevented library use. One faculty member with an outstanding teaching reputation at a large institution inquired, "How do you send 600 students to the library?" Another asked, "Who wants to read 100 term papers?" "Sometimes," commented one, "when dealing with a large number of students, it is simpler to assign the textbook."

Others underestimated the skills involved in using an academic library. They remained convinced "students learn how to use the library in the freshman year through tours given by the library staff." Many maintained, "Students can learn how to use the library through trial and error—just as I did. The library is not so complicated that someone who wants to use it can quickly learn how. No special effort is required."

One faculty member, however, candidly stated, "I had to get over the notion that as a professional person I should already know how to use the library." Another admitted, "The library can have a threatening role to the teacher." Perhaps for this reason, yet another recommended, "Librarians could increase library use through workshops and other outreach programs to the faculty." "For librarians to increase use of the library they need to change the faculty members," recommended a faculty member. "The library suffers because of lack of creativity of teachers in designing use of the library," acknowledged another faculty member.

Why are faculty members not trained better to teach? Faculty culture holds that an individual only needs training in subject matter to become a college teacher (Eble, 1972). A common view is individuals who have shown academic competence in a subject area will be successful in communicating their knowledge in the classroom (Gurland, 1978). Wilson et al. (1975), for example, quoted a university faculty member who commented, "We try to hire the best authority on the subject, and he is by definition the best teacher of the subject" (p. 23). As a result, graduate faculty, educating the next generation of faculty, must provide evidence of research ability. They, however, seldom have to provide evidence of teaching ability (Blau, 1973).

Frequently, a bias exists in graduate education against formal training in pedagogy (Eble, 1983). Academic tradition holds that "a teacher is born, not made." "Teaching is an art, not a science" (Gaff, 1975, p. 91). Graduate education exposes relatively few prospective faculty members to courses in learning theory, course design, and practical teaching (Carnegie Foundation, 1977). Faculty members are often skeptical, even snobbish, towards educationalists and pedagogy (Riesman, 1975). Many faculty members remain unconvinced that educationalists know much about successful teaching (Mayhew & Ford, 1971).

Newman (1985) remarked that graduate education of most faculty members involves risk avoidance. Few undertake unusual or interdisciplinary dissertations. Even fewer seek formal study in pedagogy. The result is that graduate study prepares faculty members to be professional economists, physicists, or whatever. It seldom prepares them to be undergraduate teachers (Project on Redefining, 1985).

Once in their positions, faculty members often receive little encouragement in the development of their teaching skills. Fink (1982) noted that most new faculty members feel inadequately supported by colleges. Few institutions routinely give new faculty members the light teaching loads that favor the development of teaching skills. Their new responsibilities often created beleaguered novice instructors. They look for any help available. One young faculty member we interviewed expressed considerable appreciation for the guidance and structure provided by a librarian while the faculty member served as a teaching assistant.

Even more experienced faculty members seldom help each other. Academic freedom has become interwoven with the sanctity of the classroom.

Many faculty members consider it somehow unprofessional for one to criticize, offer suggestions, or even observe others in their classrooms (Gaff, 1975). The faculty member's teaching is not open to the scrutiny of peers except most indirectly and unreliably (Shils, 1979). One faculty member commented to us that professors are loners. They do not want to work with others. As a result, he declared, faculty members often do not know what precedes their courses nor what follows.

Freedman et al. (1979) noted that faculty members seldom even talk about their teaching or a philosophy of education. He found, "Faculty approach teaching and education as would any intelligent adult chosen at random—on the basis of some opinion and reading and some knowledge based on experience" (p. 8). Some observers have highly condemned this lack of preparation. The authors of *Integrity in the College Curriculum* wrote, "If the professional preparation of doctors were as minimal as that of college teachers, the United States would have more funeral directors than lawyers" (Project on Redefining, 1985, p. 35).

As a result of their indifferent prepartion for teaching undergraduates, faculty members usually reproduce or recreate their own education experiences (Gurland, 1978). Most faculty members emphasize subject matter in their teaching. They assume that students learn through exposure to the right subject matter. This includes attending lectures, doing the reading assignments, and perhaps working in the library (Astin, 1985).

Riesman et al. (1971) described these faculty members as didactic teachers. They wrote:

> A didactic teacher takes for granted his greater knowledge and authority, and invites students into the materials in terms set by him. The class is a production in which the instructor is the producer, the director, and the writer, while the students are the actors under his direction and also the ultimate audience. At the very least, what is asked of them is that they "get the material." (pp. 120–121)

These faculty members conceive of education as filling "empty vessels" with "the truth" (Finkelstein, 1984, p. 107). Finkelstein (1984) found "student mastery of knowledge in a discipline and development of the ability to think clearly" (p. 106) the most important teaching goal of undergraduate faculty members.

Freedman et al. (1979) noted that a major concern for many faculty members is whether their teaching meets professional standards of rigor and content. This, he concluded, "Often results in professors regarding the function of their teaching as being primarily informational, that is, communicating to their students certain knowledge and techniques dominant in their profession" (p. 20).

Several faculty members we interviewed commented, "It is unrewarding to have students use the library in relation to other things we want to teach them." An exasperated professor stated, "I just try to get through the concepts of the discipline." One professor, however, remarked, "There is limited time in the classroom, and I use the library as one method of continuing education."

At the university level, faculty members employ a teaching method that involves lectures and detail notes (Wilson et al., 1975). Even at the college level, much of the learning is passive. Chickering (1969) found students spent a large portion of their time listening and memorizing with less emphasis on analyzing, synthesizing, applying, or evaluating. McKeachie (1962) commented:

> College teaching and lecturing have been so long been associated that when one pictures a college professor in a classroom, he almost inevitably pictures him as lecturing. The popularity of the lecture probably derives from a conception of the instructor's primary goal as that of transmitting knowledge. (p. 320).

Eble (1972) reported the lecture as the most common mode of instruction at any given time for almost any teacher. He wrote, "In my visits I encountered very little teaching which did not fit this pattern" (p. 8).

There may be other reasons for the popularity of the lecture. We interviewed a young faculty member who suggested, "The easiest way to teach is to lecture, have multiple choice tests, and avoid personal contact with the students." Rudolph (1977), a strong critic of the lecture, concluded, "The lecture . . . stretched the distance between teacher and student" (p. 232). Nevertheless, historically the lecture has become the device that paid for the seminar and small classes. Rudolph (1977) asserted that the economic theory of education management firmly grounds itself in the lecture.

Wilson et al. (1975) concluded that institutional norms do affect teaching style. University faculty tended to be more subject- oriented while community college faculty tended to be more student-oriented. At the university level, faculty members expect students to be highly dedicated to seeking knowledge. Faculty members place intellectual quality above student needs.

Students cannot succeed in the system if they fail to meet the standards defined by the faculty. Faculty members require the student to adjust to their standards. Finkelstein (1984) concluded that faculty members only marginally adjust their teaching based on student feedback and inservice training. "Too many students," however, a faculty member deplored to us, "are unwilling to meet the standards." Faculty members often mentioned to us the lack of student interest and commitment. One remarked, "Students have a great tendency to complain."

Faculty members often assume because they teach, students learn (Newman, 1985). They believe that students wishing to learn should seek the faculty members (Eble, 1983). One faculty member, however, admitted, "It is sobering to see how little gets across to students." Another described it as "scary to discover how little students know."

The subject-matter approach, whereby the faculty member lectures to the uninformed student, clearly favors the highly motivated students (Astin, 1985). Jencks and Riesman (1968) found that many faculty members want undergraduates to act like graduate apprentices, both socially and intellectually. Several faculty members we interviewed expressed the view, "If students are not majors in my discipline then there is no use to introduce them to the literature of the discipline." Others commented, "Use of the library is more appropriate as students get into graduate school." Many we interviewed, however, did not see the need for a separate track for majors and nonmajors.

Nevertheless, Riesman et al. (1971) found that faculty members often direct their teaching somewhere above the median of class ability. Sometimes faculty members aim their instruction only to the top two or three students. Only rarely do they teach to the slowest or least attentive students. One faculty member we met declared, "The library is really intended for the brightest and most motivated students. It is not surprising that most students do not use the library or most of the materials are not used."

Faculty members themselves were good students, and as graduate students they always associated with other good students (Astin, 1985). They value the demonstration of intellect over the development of intellect (Astin, 1985). They are reluctant to deal with the unprepared student. Several faculty members during our interviews complained about student abilities. They did not believe is should be necessary to "lead students by the hand to the library." One declared it is "up to the students—either sink or swim."

Faculty members frequently assume that individuals who stand at the top of one measure of talent will probably also stand at the top of any other socially important talent. That is, those undergraduates who make good grades in college will turn out to be the ones who have talent in other areas and who become successful in life (Cross, 1976). Only these students merit the faculty member's time. Some faculty members we interviewed indicated that they had different standards for the "better students."

Research, however, repeatedly has shown the inaccuracy of the myth that grades predict success in later life. McClelland (1973) reviewed the literature in the early 1970s and concluded, "Researchers have in fact had great difficulty demonstrating that grades in school are related to any other behaviors of importance—other than doing well on aptitude tests" (p. 2).

Faculty members also often believe that students should put major, if not exclusive, emphasis on academic work. Faculty members speak of "learning for its own sake." For example, on several occasions we had faculty members express the view that "students should learn how to use the library for its own sake." Declared one professor, "We love books and students should love books."

"Learning for its own sake," however, is a concept foreign to many students (Riesman et al., 1971). "To many students," a sociologist explained to us, "the library is an abstraction." Several faculty members reported, "It is difficult to get students to do things for their own good, such as use the library." Many faculty members complained of student pragmatism and narrow focus.

Students set their own priorities among the areas of activities available (Becker, Geer, & Hughes, 1968). For example, Becker et al. (1968) found most students' bookshelves contained nothing but textbooks. They concluded that many students had little use for books not helpful in meeting requirements. Perhaps this is why one faculty member declared, "Librarians pushing things onto students does not really have that much effect." Others, perhaps understanding the student view, complained, "Librarians try to introduce too much. They need to cut down on information and concentrate on what is needed." One, perhaps recognizing the connection between requirements and library use, declared, "Librarians will not reach the students independent of courses."

Many faculty members wanted to believe that undergraduates do not learn because of lack of opportunties. For example, several faculty members wanted their institution's library open 24 hours a day so the students could get to it. A few, however, then admitted that students could get to the library without expanding the hours if the students really want to do so. An experienced professor commented, "Later library hours merely allows students to come in later." Sometimes undergraduates have different priorities despite the hopes of faculty members.

In our interviews, many faculty members talked about creating an enthusiasm for learning. Several mentioned enticing students into learning to enjoy using the library—often in lieu of specific assignments. In fact, one faculty member specifically mention a distaste for a "reward and condition approach to education."

"Librarians," faculty members frequently stated in our interviews, "should be friendly, receptive, and infinitely patient." Librarians should encourage browsing. "People need to see things on the shelf so they will be encourage to read them," recommended a faculty member. Several mentioned that the library should be quiet. Many faculty expressed a desire for an inviting atmosphere in the library. The library should have soft chairs, bright colors, open spaces, and nice places to study.

A few even suggested that the ethos of the library is more important than the size of its collection. Many, however, subscribed to the resource view of teaching. That is, student learning will occur if administrators bring adequate resources together in one place. The more resources there are, the better learning is (Astin, 1985). In their view, the larger the library the better it will serve undergraduate education. Corollary to this view is the belief that recruitment of more high-achieving students will result in more library use.

There are reasons, however, for students not to follow too closely faculty expectations. Astin (1985) found heavy academic involvement sometimes holds back those changes in personality and behavior that normally result from college attendance. He found the only personality change strengthened by academic involvement is the need for status. A network of student culture and social arrangements filters faculty influence on students (Becker et al., 1968). In fact, students' interests outside the prescribed curriculum have given many desirable features to the college scene, including libraries, dramatics, music, and speech (Mayhew & Ford, 1971).

Gaff (1983) concluded that the faculty members who had the greatest impact on undergraduates differed from other faculty members in several ways. These faculty members expressed more interest in teaching than in research and in teaching undergraduates than graduate students. They talked much more with students about a variety of issues important to young adults of the day. He found the extent to which they interacted with students outside the classroom the biggest single difference between influential faculty members and their colleagues. In our interviews, we found considerable evidence of these kinds of teachers.

Wilson et al. (1975), however, also found that many faculty members hold highly favorable, possibly exaggerated, views of their teaching. Faculty members develop their teaching methods through a complex interaction of institutional norms, individual faculty goals, values, interests, and intellectual competencies. Their teaching methods have evolved over the course of an academic career. They are not readily changed.

SUMMARY

Higher education faculty members play a very important role in American society. Nevertheless, we found contemporary faculty culture disquieting. Faculty members live in a culture fraught with contradictions and inconsistencies. Their values and interests simultaneously pull them in different directions. Graduate education socializes them to values often incompatible with the later circumstances. In a culture that prizes knowledge and reflection, faculty members often find themselves ill-prepared and with little time for their daily responsibilities.

Graduate study encourages potential faculty members to specialize and to do research in a specific subject area. While inclined in this direction even as undergraduates, they come to value scholarship and intellectual pursuits even more. Typically, however, departmental chairpersons and deans assign beginning faculty members to teach lower division and general education classes. Reaching and inspiring indifferent undergraduates is frequently exhausting and unrewarding. At this level, faculty members often find their research skills irrelevant and their teaching skills underdeveloped. As they seek membership in the community of scholars, faculty members receive little help from their colleagues.

Scholarship teaches them the importance of time to reflect, to ponder, and to deliberate. Their daily responsibilities, however, drain them of their time. Students unresponsive to their love of knowledge and areas of specialty weaken their enthusiasms. Publication requirements forces them to "bore towards tenure" as the price of permanent membership in the academic community. Continued vigilance in defending academic freedoms and professional prerogatives further depletes their stamina.

While they spend most of their time teaching, research provides the most tangible rewards. Institutions demand their time, but their loyalties lie with their discipline, which provides mobility, prestige, and security. Departments protect and reward them but isolate them from colleagues. Academic freedom supports their autonomy and the sanctity of the classroom. It also thwarts potentially supportive relationships with colleagues.

Nevertheless, most faculty members do enjoy their profession. They report teaching and working with students as major sources of satisfaction. Most want to be evaluated more on their teaching than their research. We found many who provided considerable evidence that they worked hard at teaching.

We, however, sensed that academic culture also obstructs integration of the academic library into undergraduate education. While many faculty members engaged their students in use of the academic library, we found others indifferent or even resistant. Undergraduate use of the library demands more of faculty members than many are able or willing to give.

Their miscalculation of the skills and incentives needed to use the academic library deflects a perceived need for systematic library instruction. As with many of their teaching skills, faculty members developed their library skills through trial and error. They think undergraduates can do the same—forgetting that most undergraduates neither share their abilities nor their motivations. Their isolation from colleagues inhibits progressive and sequential development of library skills.

Many faculty members reserve library use for only the brightest and most inspired students. They believe only these students can appreciate and will join the "invitation to learn." Faculty members enjoy the accumulation of knowledge. They look for students who share their values. They do not understand students who do not share this love of learning.

Faculty members often suggest the library should somehow entice students into loving books—as they love books. They often conclude that the library would be more central to the academic enterprise only with better students, more books, and longer hours. Structured assignments that require undergraduates to use the library seemed foreign to the spirit of learning for many faculty members.

As faculty members seek courses in which to teach their specialties, they seek additional library resources. These demands often strain the library's time and resources. Faculty members often do not want to commit their energies to select materials. Their time constraints and loyalties to the discipline make them doubt the worth of spending time to develop local resources. On the other hand, they often will not relinquish to librarians the opportunity to make selections. Their subject specialization encourages them to think only they can do it. Unfortunately, many useful library materials remain unacquired and many acquired items remain unused. Perhaps, given contemporary faculty culture, we should be amazed that undergraduates use the library as much as they do.

chapter nine

WORKING WITH FACULTY*

INTRODUCTION

The academic library remains an underutilized resource in undergraduate education. Several recent writers on higher education have commented on its lack of use. Eble (1983) wrote, "Libraries have never been fully integrated into the teaching program despite their long existence at the center of the college campus" (p. 172). Boyer (1987) found the library "underfunded and underused" (p. 292). He concluded that the "gap between the classroom and the library, reported almost half a century ago, still exists" (p. 161).

Boyer (1987) supported his conclusion with the following evidence:

> Today, about one out of every four undergraduates spends no time in the library during a normal week, and 65 percent use the library four hours or less each week. Nearly one quarter reported spending just one to two hours there each week. This means that about half of all the undergraduate students spend no more than two hours in the library each week.
>
> We found that the library is viewed by most undergraduates simply as a quiet place to study. (pp. 160–161)

Boyer (1987) recommended that every undergraduate receives bibliographic instruction and spend at least as much time in the library as they spend in classes.

To accomplish this, Boyer (1987) called for librarians who understand and are involved in educational matters. We add to this a call for librarians who understand faculty members and seek to work with them. We believe that only through librarians working with faculty members will the library become fully integrated into undergraduate education. Understanding and working with faculty members, however, is frequently a challenge.

---

* Portions of this chapter were previously published as Hardesty, L. (1979). Instructional Development in Library Use Education. In C. A. Kirkendall (Ed.), *Improving Library Instructions: How to Teach and How to Evaluate* (pp. 11–35). Ann Arbor, MI: Pierian.

RESISTANCE TO CHANGE

Faculty members have become well-known for their resistance to change. They are more liberal and willing to embrace change in society than in their own institutions (Wilson et al., 1975). Astin (1985) noted that the attitude of faculty members sometimes "takes the form of blind resistance to almost any change" (p. 197). This inherent conservatism among faculty often leads to an atmosphere of institutional pessimism (Astin, 1985). "Changing the curriculum," wrote Hefferlin (1971), "is like moving a graveyard" (p. 18). Supporters must consider the feelings of everyone even remotely related with the undertaking (Hefferlin, 1971). Jencks and Riesman (1968) concluded, "Faculty members have an extraordinarily skewed perception of their own behavior, both individual and collective, and have little sense that their demands are often 'impossible' " (p. 18).

Historically, many reasons exist for this conservatism. Faculties can become isolated. Rudolph (1977) proclaimed, "Assemble a cluster of professors in a country town, surround them with scenic grandeur, cut them off from the world beyond, and they will not have much trouble congratulating themselves into curricular torpor" (p. 3). On the other hand, most faculty members have become more cosmopolitan and transferred their loyalties to their discipline. With this change, they may have abandoned the sense of corporate responsibility that characterized faculty members of earlier days (Project on Redefining, 1985). Perhaps the continual struggles of faculties to withstand the demands of business, religious, or government groups also have encouraged conservatism (Sanford, 1962).

Other factors come into play. Faculty culture treats the faculty member as an independent professional. Astin (1985) concluded, "Faculty members probably have more personal and professional autonomy than any other group of professionals employed in structured organizations" (p. 197). Clark (1987) stated his conclusions more strongly. He commented, "We cannot help but be struck by the virtual rights so many academics seem to possess to go their own way, simply assuming they can do largely as they please a good share of the time, all in the nature of rational behavior" (p. 148). Astin (1985) noted, "Naturally, faculty members value their autonomy highly and guard vigilantly against attempts to limit it" (p. 197).

Particularly after they have achieved tenure, Hefferlin (1971) concluded, there is little beyond persuasion to change faculty members attitudes and behaviors about their responsibilities. In addition, because of the norms of faculty culture, typically faculty members make little effort to persuade each other to change. Each seems willing to let others alone.

Faculty members usually are busy with their teaching and scholarly responsibilities. Many studies show that faculty members work far beyond the 40-hour-week (Bowen & Schuster, 1986). Therefore, they are likely to resent and oppose proposals for change that require more of their time (Astin, 1985). Early in their careers most spent considerable time in developing instructional strategies they consider effective and consistent with their personal styles. Once developed, many faculty members reluctantly change their teaching methods (Carnegie Foundation, 1977).

Despite their independence, Bowen and Schuster (1986) found that many faculty members perceived a considerable erosion of their autonomy and of participation in institutional decision making. This may be the response of threatened and insecure individuals. Change can be threatening, and an insecure person reacts defensively to threats (Mayhew & Ford, 1971). Faculty members may even view requiring change in them as a violation of academic freedom (Hefferlin, 1971).

Changes in curriculum can take away much of the significance of an individual's life work. It is little wonder that such changes are unwelcome (Woodburne, 1958). Cross (1976) suggested that traditional disciplines now may be facing problems similar to those met by the classical curriculum around the turn of the century. Perhaps these changes are the erosion in autonomy that many faculty members perceive.

Faculty governance and decision making also leads to considerable conservatism about change. Jencks and Riesman (1968) found faculty members "neither a tolerant nor an easy-going species" (p. 17). Faculty members frequently judge that they alone are competent to decide on curricular and other areas affecting them. They often regard administrators with "fear, suspicion, and contempt" (Astin, 1985, p. 197). They perceive administrators as not sharing their values. Faculty members typically presume administrators as possibly failed faculty members who value power and authority over teaching and scholarship. They view administrators as potential threats to their autonomy (Astin, 1985). In the faculty view, administrators should serve foremost as facilitators. Administrators should provide "money, facilities, conveniences, and services" (Martin, 1968, p. 97) necessary for the faculty members.

Levine and Weingart (1973) found that despite low institutional loyalty, faculty members fear administrators will leave them out of governance decisions. Faculty members do not want to run the college and few enjoy the process. Nevertheless, few are willing to leave it to someone else (Eble, 1972). As a result, they insist on serving on such trivial committees as "student housing, parking, or dining" (Eble, 1972, p. 134). Service on these committees deeply cut into their time.

Perhaps more important, academic governance is often ineffective. Faculty committees typically do not seek information to solve problems. They try to form a consensus (Levine & Weingart, 1973). Decision making by consensus provides considerable power to individual faculty members. Even if most faculty members support an idea, one recalcitrant individual can often wield inordinate negative power (Astin, 1985). Therefore, Hefferlin (1971) concluded, turnover in personnel, a slow process, is more central to academic reform than to change in other organizations.

Graduate school, furthermore, has socialized faculty members as skeptics (Bess, 1982b). Graduate school rewards prospective faculty members for displaying their critical abilities. They have years of practice before joining their profession. Those who do not show adequate critical skills seldom become faculty members. Wrote Astin (1985):

Little wonder, then, that the tendency to display one's superior critical ability by finding fault should carry over into faculty life or that the initial faculty reaction to any proposal for change is an analysis of its defects. (p. 198)

When skepticism and suspicion are combined with governance through consensus seeking, we find a strong disposition to resist change.

Faculty members, while recognizing the difficulty of change, tend to blame other factors than themselves. Wrote Astin (1985):

When pushed to account for institutional inertia, faculty members often cite the cumbersome administrative structure or even the conservatism and obstreperousness of their own colleagues. They are unable or unwilling to face the fact that they personally contribute to the inertia: through their mistrust of and even contempt for administrators and outside agencies, their blind defense of faculty autonomy, their tendency to be critical of new ideas and to display their critical skills at every possible opportunity, their passivity in the face of obstructionist colleagues, their pessimism about the prospects of significant change, and their reluctance to devote time and effort to supporting those proposals they find promising. (pp. 198–199)

We marvel how any change at all occurs in higher education.

Hefferlin (1971), however, noted that often faculty members do have good reason to resist change. At the undergraduate level, they must offer programs to attract clientele of both adequate numbers and acceptable abilities. On the other hand, they must respond to the expectations of employers and graduate schools. Caught between, radical changes in any direction can result in a loss of a hard earned reputation and economic disaster. In any case, commented Hefferlin (1971), seldom in higher education do innovations make reputations.

Levine and Weingart (1973) concluded that the answer to change lies not in reproaching the faculty members. The solution lies in changing society and the rewards it offers. Levine (1978) found within faculty a strong sentiment for change. He noted, "Forty-four percent of American faculty believe that the undergraduate curriculum at their college or university is in serious need of reform" (p. 425). Wilson et al. (1975) also found a

strong sentiment for change among individual faculty members. Nevertheless, the factors we have discussed explain why faculties resist change. Librarians need to draw upon the sentiments for change among individual
faculty members.

DIFFUSION AND ADOPTION OF INNOVATION

We may live in an age of unprecedented change. Nevertheless, securing
the acceptance of a new idea or the adoption of an innovation often is
difficult. In the commercial marketplace, some estimate that only one idea
out of more than every 500 results in a successful new product (Martin,
1964, cited in Rogers, 1971). Only about 8 percent of the more than 6,000
new consumer products introduced each year have a life expectancy of
even one year (Conner, cited in Rogers, 1971). Innovations whether they
be in business, agriculture, education, or librarianship often have a short life.
Individuals may adopted them only after many years of struggle.

Education contains many examples of the struggles involved in gaining
the acceptance of an innovation. Cross (1976) noted, "Curricular changes
are made ever so slowly" (p. 20). For example, George Washington proposed in his second presidential message including agricultural study in
the curriculum of a national university. Nevertheless, Congress took nearly
100 years to get the message that formal learning could improve farming
(Cross, 1976).

Kindergarten is another example. After its initial introduction into the
United States, more than 50 years lapsed before schools widely adopted it
during the 1930s and 1940s. In fact, some experts estimate that the public
education has a 50-year time lag. Some experts predict that not until about
the year 2000 will schools widely adopt elements of the post-World War
II educational reform movement (Glines, 1973). As we approach that year,
even this estimate seems optimistic.

Even with the educational crisis created by Sputnik many schools remain virtually untouched by the huge federal and state expenditures promoting educational reform during the past 30 years. For example, during
the 1960s and 1970s the Council on Library Resources and the National
Endowment for the Humanities provided more than three million dollars
for bibliographic instruction. Nevertheless, Gwinn (1980) found at the end
of the 1970s few bibliographic instructional programs had become institutionalized.

House (1974) asked the question, "How can so much effort directed
toward changing the school produce so little change?" (p. 2). Romey
(1977) compared educational institutions with blobs of gelatin. They ab-
sorb efforts to change their shapes. New programs sometimes make dents,

but soon afterwards the institution springs back to its original shape. The influence of the innovation disappears without a trace.

The diversity of faculty members and distinctiveness of institutional situations make it difficult to generalize from other experiences. Nevertheless, information from the literature on the diffusion and adoption of innovations provides some direction. Researchers have conducted studies on topics as diverse as planting new varieties of crops to prescribing new drugs.

Research on the diffusion of innovations dates back to the 1930s. Notable early studies include the investigation of the use of hybrid corn in Iowa. The real growth spurt of diffusion studies, however, began in the 1950s. A continued expansion of the number of diffusion publications continues to the present. Despite their complexity, "To a certain extent, all diffusion studies looked a great deal alike" (Radnor, Feller, & Rogers, 1978, p. 2).

While we may talk about living in a rapidly changing world, resistance to change is natural and often desireable. Watson (1969) noted, "All the forces which contribute to stability in personality or in social systems can be perceived as resisting change" (p. 488). Without some level of resistance, there would be no stability. Our lives would soon become intolerable if we accepted every new idea or fad that came along.

Research has shown that a plan for promoting change is an essential ingredient for a successful change effort. In an important study of major innovative projects in education conducted during the past 75 years, the authors concluded, "A change initiated in a particular school, in the absence of a plan . . . is not likely to become widely or firmly entrenched" (Orlosky & Smith, 1972, p. 414).

Research shows that change agents should consider several factors in a plan for promoting a particular change. A change agent needs to consider (a) the characteristics of the innovation itself, (b) the social system in which the change agent promotes innovation, and (c) the process through which individuals accept or reject the innovation, including useful strategies for promoting change within this process. Even before we consider these factors, however, we need to consider librarians' roles as change agents.

The Change Agent

Change agents should first examine their own motives before embarking on a campaign to change the behavior and ideas of others. Wrote Palmatier (1975), change agents who seek to:

> gain personal attention, dramatize differences between themselves and others, and criticize and attack the system can be sure they will program themselves open and hostile opposition. They are their own best enemies. (p. 60)

The successful change agent often is one who promotes change quietly and without fanfare.

Too often change agents exhibit a "true believer" syndrome. Problems can develop with high expectations and unrealistic plans. Unreasonable ambitions inevitably doom these plans to some degree of failure. Sometimes change agents exhibit an overpowering urgency to start a program with little or no planning. They often express this attitude as "Let's get started and we'll find out just what we're doing as we go along" (Kritek, 1976, p. 90).

In listing the desirable characteristics of change agents, researchers usually include such characteristics as patience, willingness to work hard, and courage. Change agents need these attributes to help overcome fantasies and stereotypes. They must build the necessary confidence for them to offer help and for potential adopters to accept it (Evans, 1968).

Researchers have noted that change agents must be careful in committing their time and energy. Potential adopters drop many innovations when the promoters "burn out." Too often change efforts begin with a flurry of activity. They last only a year or so, however, because the individuals involved cannot maintain the pace to which they have committed themselves (Kritek, 1976). Change agents need to maintain a delicate balance. They must have enough enthusiasm to maintain the change effort in the face of resistance and not so much enthusiasm that they overlook careful planning.

The Innovation and the Adopter

The characteristics of an innovation are significant. Seldom, however, do potential adopters accept a change just because it might be a good idea. In fact, the actual characteristics of an innovation may have little impact on the adoption of the innovation. Miles (1964) concluded individuals seldom accept educational innovations on their own merits. He found, "Characteristics of the local system, of the innovating person or group, and of other relevant groups, often outweigh the impact of what the innovation is" (p. 635). How potential adopters view the innovation is more important than how the change agent views it.

Schein and Bennis (1965) reported that people usually do not change as a result of information. Individuals ignore things they do not like to hear, discount the validity of the information, or attribute the problem to something outside of themselves. Often administrators become ready scapegoats for faculty members (Jencks & Riesman, 1968). Schein and Bennis (1965) found:

> If the cues are the least bit ambiguous, we can easily dismiss them; if the cues are too blunt, we can attempt to dismiss the person who provided them;

if we cannot evade the message at all, we can still rationalize the behavior which triggered the disconfirmatory cue as not being, after all, characteristic of our own typical behavior, and so on. (p. 278)

Attitude change, they determined, is more than providing disconfirmatory cues.

Schein and Bennis (1965) reported attitude change requires both heightened anxiety and reduction of threat. They found:

A person cannot learn about himself and others in a group unless he gets certain categories of information which are not readily available. And, he cannot get these categories of information unless his attitudes change about which kinds of data are relevant, which data he is willing to reveal about himself and which data he is willing to pay attention to in others. To put it even more concretely, the learning process at the outset hinges upon a person's becoming willing and able to reveal his own feelings and reactions, and upon his becoming willing and able to listen and pay attention to the feelings and reactions of others. (p. 273)

They found the attitudes about the learning process as quite central to the person and integrated with self-concept. Individuals strongly hold attitudes in this area and resist their change. Several faculty members we interviewed reported that the library can have a threatening role to them. "The library," one confided, "is a constant reminder to produce."

Some faculty members, for example, do not believe that many undergraduates neither use nor know how to use the academic library. These faculty members may strongly resist the idea that students seldom, if ever, use many library materials. The response of some faculty members to the Pittsburgh library study of the 1970s provides evidence of this reaction (Borkowski & MacLeod, 1979a, 1979b, 1979c).

Schein and Bennis (1965) commented on the need to create a climate of psychological safety for change to occur. They wrote individuals seldom immediately drop their defenses in the face of change. Individuals must feel assured that others value them enough to help them to change. Individuals must feel protected during the sometimes painful process of change. Watson (1969) found that change agents can reduce resistance to change if they can empathize with potential adopters. Change agents must recognize legitimate objections and take steps to relieve unnecessary concerns.

Eble (1983) concluded that educational reformers should take a low key approach with faculty. Change agents should downplay the need and not greatly advertise the availability of help. Participation should be strictly a matter of faculty member's own choosing. Faculty members must acknowledge need before change can occur.

Understanding faculty culture should help librarians to promote further library use. Faculty members seldom discuss their teaching with their colleagues. Librarians, however, can serve as nonevaluative (and nonthreatening) respondents to faculty members. Through careful guidance librarians can evoke change among the faculty.

Promotion of Change

Rogers (1971) has written the most comprehensive book available on promotion and adoption of new ideas, *Communication of Innovation*. In this book he reported his scrutiny of literally hundreds of studies on the adoption of new ideas. He classified the perceived characteristics of innovations that affect their adoption.

Relative Advantage.
Rogers (1971) defined relative advantage as "the degree to which an innovation is perceived by the adopter as better than the idea it supersedes. The greater the perceived relative advantage of an innovation, the more rapid its rate of adoption" (pp. 22–23). Relative advantage includes considerations such as will the innovation increase the teaching load, increase the time needed to grade papers, or increase the time needed for class preparation and research.

Most faculty members probably view bibliographic instruction in a different perspective than do librarians. As already noted, Knapp (1966b) concluded from her experience:

> Most college faculty members see library instruction as dealing with bits of information, undeniably useful, but fragmented, not related to any single, coherent framework, not calling for problem-solving behavior, for critical thinking, for imagination. (p. 89)

Many faculty members we interviewed asked, "Why should I bother with something that means more work . . . why should I go through the hassle?" Several recommended released time from teaching to encourage more student use of the library.

Compatibility.
Rogers (1971) defined compatibility as "the degree to which an innovation is perceived by the adopter as being consistent with existing values, past experiences, and the needs of the receivers" (pp. 22–23). Eble (1972) noted, "There remain difficulties in getting faculty members to enter into teaching arrangements which may violate their personal beliefs about the privacy of the classroom and which may require more classroom manage-

ment" (p. 149). Levine and Weingart (1973) commented on the difficulty of bringing about interdisciplinary and team-taught programs. The discipline orientation and sanctity of the classroom work against their acceptance of these programs.

Many faculty members do not view librarians as colleagues and fellow educators. Some view librarians as a special kind of administrator—as facilitators and providers of service. These faculty members, therefore, judge librarians, as they do administrators, by their ability to provide the money, facilities, conveniences, and services faculty members have decreed necessary for a professional environment (Martin, 1968, p. 97).

For instance, faculty members frequently view librarians as service providers (Oberg, Schleiter, & Van Houten, 1989). One faculty member we interviewed strongly stated, "Professionalism of librarians has resulted in segregation of librarians from clientele. Professionalization has led away from knowing the collection." He asserted, "The notes and information sent faculty are self-serving and used to justify the professionalization of librarians—half of it is garbage." Many faculty members interviewed did not expect the librarians to know more about the materials of their disciplines.

Many faculty members held that librarians and students need very little skill to uncover tertiary and secondary material. Several faculty members held as a major concern that librarians need to get books back on shelves where the books belong. These faculty members also insisted that they, not the librarians, should teach students writing and critical thinking skills.

A few faculty members, however, acknowledged that librarians know more about how students use the library than do faculty members. These faculty members viewed a major function of librarians as keeping faculty aware of new sources. They expressed appreciation for the interdisciplinary approach of librarians.

Even more positive, a faculty member at Earlham College declared, "I am uncomfortable with notion of library as a service place." He held, "Librarians are colleagues instead of people who deliver a service." Several of his colleagues at this college expressed similar views. One stated, "Librarians are an active part of the educational process—not just curators of books."

The Earlham faculty members held librarians to high standards. Stated another faculty member, "Librarians need to perform in the classroom at the same level of teaching as the rest of the faculty. They must be articulate and dynamic. They must sell a message." This supports Oberg's et al. (1989) recent conclusion. Increased contact between librarians and faculty members enhances the status of the librarians in the eyes of the faculty members.

Many faculty members hold uncertain attitudes toward librarians. Their responses to statement 15 on the attitude scale provide further evidence of this ambivalence. This statement reads: Librarians should have advanced degrees in other disciplines in addition to a degree in library science if they are to help students use the library. About one-quarter of the respondents circled the undecided response. Their responses to this question did not correlate with the responses to the rest of the attitude scale (see Appendix A).

This same response held true in the interviews. Some faculty members stated, "We need more specialists in the library with Ph.D.s in subject fields." Such librarians, they held, "could better understand the nature of the literature and the research of a field or discipline. It would reduce distance between teaching and research." Some faculty members interviewed believed "Librarians should have to teach and publish to understand our problems."

Others see librarians as providers of a service and increased professionalization (and increased degrees) as a disadvantage to the faculty. Other faculty members remained undecided as to their attitudes toward librarians. We concluded that many faculty members more readily accepted librarians as colleagues when librarians more nearly fit the traditional faculty mode. When librarians do not, faculty members often have trouble perceiving librarians as colleagues. We found an unclear relationship between attitudes of faculty members toward the undergraduate educational role of the library and their attitudes toward the need for advance degrees for librarians (see Appendix A).

Bibliographic instruction also may not be compatible with other values and experiences held by instructors. It tends to be process oriented while many classroom instructors tend to empathize the accumulation of knowledge. Bibliographic instruction may be more student-oriented than discipline-oriented faculty members welcome.

From instructional development, several patterns have emerged about teacher acceptance of methods of instruction. Teachers often resist instructional methods which result in their having less control over the classroom and the student. Teachers also resist change that may lessen their position as authorities in the subject. They do not want to be placed in a vulnerable position of having to learn about another's field (Morrish, 1976). As one faculty member admitted, "I had to get over the notion that I as a professional person should know how to use the library." As Eble (1983) concluded, "Most people resist being taught what they already think they know" (p. 134).

Knapp (1966b) found that often faculty members believed that all instruction about bibliographic work should be done by them, or that it was the province of the faculty members—not librarians—to recommend sources of information. One faculty member we interviewed admitted that he liked control over his classes and what they read. He remarked, "Lots of stuff is not worth reading."

Another clear pattern is that frequently teachers will not fully accept certain methods of instruction because of their definitions of teaching. Researchers determined that instructors often define teaching as capturing and holding the attention of students, and serving as the continuous mediator between students and information. Evans (1968) found that many teachers resisted instructional television. They viewed it as lacking the ingredients of personal contact between teaching and students, feedback from students, and proper supervision of students.

Instructors emphasize those elements of an instructional method that are most compatible with their experience and values. They de-emphasize the elements that are not (Kritek, 1976). In a major study on programmed learning, Carlson (1965) reported that a group of teachers viewed programmed learning as a threat to their concept of teaching. They consciously or unconsciously did several things to counter its effectiveness. The developers created programmed instruction to let students work at their own rate, but the teachers involved in the study prevented this. Thorough various methods they restricted the faster students and allowed the slower students to keep pace. In the end, the programmed instruction method began to look very similar to traditional instructional methods.

Complexity.
Rogers (1971) defined complexity as "the degree to which an innovation is perceived as difficult to understand and use" (p. 23). Evans (1968) traced the high rate of failure of audio-visual programs to the issue of complexity. Teachers had to exert considerable effort to use the equipment.

Other researchers attributed the success or failure of several of the major curriculum reform efforts during the 1960s to the degree of complexity. The American physics curriculum reform of that decade had a slow rate of adoption. It had a materials-centered approach, but the developers had no deliberate plan of providing materials to the teachers. On the other hand, teachers widely adopted the science and mathematics programs developed by the National Science Foundation. Its developers created the programs as complete units for use by individual teachers (Morrish, 1976).

Librarians must consider how well classroom instructors understand what we mean by bibliographic instruction. Do librarians require faculty members to learn new skills? How much effort do they need to continue bibliographic instruction? Some researchers note that change agents must lessen resistance to an innovation based on a lack of understanding. They should try to bring participants into the diagnostic efforts leading them to agree on what the basic problems are and their importance (Watson, 1969).

Trialability.
Rogers (1971) defined trialability as "the degree to which an innovation may be experimented with on a limited basis" (p. 23). Innovations requir-

ing large expenditures of time, money, or effort by the adopting person or group usually move slowly (Miles, 1964).

Kennedy (1972) of Earlham College suggested that librarians should be like the Volkswagen people and "think small—in the beginning anyway" (p. 23). Innovations that meet this condition are those that faculty members can try on a small scale, on a partial basis, for a short time. This also refers to the number of individuals or proportion of the group required (Morrish, 1976).

Bibliographic instruction may be quite trialable with individual faculty members. Unfortunately, efforts that require progressive and sequential assignments among several faculty members are much more difficult to carry out. We found very few examples in this study of library assignments involving cooperative efforts among faculty members.

Observability.
Rogers (1971) defined observability or communicability as "the degree to which the results of an innovation are visible to others" (p. 23). One faculty member we interviewed reported that he tried bibliographic instruction "but did not see any difference afterwards." Librarians must consider how easy or how difficult it is to explain or prove the worth of undergraduate use of the library. Again, librarians must deal with perceived worth rather than what might be the actual worth. Faculty members may see a method as being less effective when research might show improved skills.

In promoting the reform of the physics curriculum during the 1960s, researchers found that teachers did not widely adopt the new syllabus where special institutes held the demonstrations and courses. Teachers, however, widely adopted the syllabus when change agents provided demonstrations and courses through model classrooms. Teachers in the local area could view the program in action (Morrish, 1976). We found it quite effective to communicate the worth of bibliographic instruction by taking faculty members to Earlham College to talk with the librarians, classroom instructors, and students.

The Social System

Characteristics of the social system or structure are a second major consideration in the promotion of an innovation. Again, Knapp (1961, 1966b) has focused the most attention to the relationship between the social structure of the academic community and the academic library. Farber (1974b) of Earlham College also has pointed out the importance of the "closely knit sense of community and very informal relations among students, faculty, administrators, and staff" (p. 145) at that institution in providing favorable conditions for bibliographic instruction.

An institution may encourage or discourage innovations. This may come through the formal reward structure such as the criteria used for tenure, promotion, and salary increases. It also may come through the way the institution encourages faculty members to interact with one another. Teaching methods, such as team teaching, allow faculty members to view each other. It may result in their supporting mutual efforts to improve their teaching by trying innovative methods. This may occur completely outside the formal reward structure of the institution.

In general, researchers emphasize the role of a few individuals in the social system. In trying any planned change, the change agent must gain legitimacy for the change through getting the support of key people (Bennis & Schein, 1969). These people are not necessarily the formal leaders of the organization (Benne & Birnbaum, 1969). They may be the "opinion leaders" because of the way they influence informally the attitudes and actions of others (Rogers, 1971). A clue for identifying opinion leaders is the extent to which other people seek them out for advice or listen attentively when they speak (Jwaideh, n.d.). Rogers (1971) found a positive relationship between the success of change agents and the extent that they work through these opinion leaders. Knapp (1966b) confirmed their importance in the Monteith College Project when she found, "The support of a powerful member of the staff could practically guarantee an initial hearing for our ideas" (p. 133).

All members of a social system usually do not adopt a new idea together. Instead, according to Rogers (1971), they adopt in "an ordered time sequence" (p. 175). Rogers (1971) classified individuals within a social system in adopter groups. He found that adopter distributions followed over time a bell-shaped curve. On the basis of their relative disposition toward innovation, he used the following groups: innovators, early adopters, early majority, late majority, and resisters.

Innovators.

These individuals are venturesome. They are the first persons in the social system to adopt an innovation. They tend to be intelligent, eager to try new ideas, and willing to take risks. They are the individuals most receptive to change. Innovators, however, tend to be individualists and usually not integrated into the dominant social structure. They seldom are opinion leaders in the social system.

There are good reason for a change agent not to work with innovators. First, they are usually too innovative to serve as models for the rest of the members of the social system. Second, innovators are often quick to drop new ideas.

Early Adopters.

This group may contain opinion leaders, depending on the social system. In fact, this adopter group, more than any other, usually has the greatest degree of opinion leadership in most social systems (Rogers, 1971). Others view these individuals as respected, knowledgeable members of the social system. Colleagues often consider the early adopter the "person to check with" before using a new idea.

Early Majority.
The members of the early majority group are deliberate. They adopt new ideas just before the average member of a social system. This group tends to be followers instead of leaders (Jwaideh, n.d.).

Late Majority.
Skeptics form the late majority group. They adopt new ideas just after the average member of the social system. Change agents can persuade them. Nevertheless, the weight of the norms of the social system must strongly favor the innovation before change agents can convince them.

Resisters.
The resisters are the last to adopt an innovation. They usually are not opinion leaders and may be almost completely isolated within the social system. By the time they adopt an innovation, other innovations may already have superseded it (Rogers, 1971). Such persons can sometimes destroy an innovative program. The change agent must try to identify them and invest extra effort to influence them or at least offset them. Members of this group often stand on tradition or existing conditions.

Change agents must identify individuals in the social system by their innovative group. With this information they know where and how to concentrate their energies and time. Identification of and work with opinion leaders are crucial. Nevertheless, one must also identify the other members of the social system in these broad groups. A change agent should be aware of the formal and informal groups in the social system. Informal groupings, such as lunch groups, are particularly important since the individuals come together voluntarily and often highly influence each other. A change agent may influence a late majority person in a desired direction if a change agent can convince an opinion leader of the same informal group to adopt an innovation.

The Individual

One model of change that emphasizes the individual is the problem-solving model. This model stresses the role of the adopter of an innovation in solving a perceived problem. A change agent may begin the change process. Nevertheless, the emphasis is on the potential adopter desiring the change and fully participating in the process of creating the change. Change agents using this model focus on the potential adopter as the starting place and the role of diagnosis in the identification of possible solutions. The change agent role is nondirective in that he or she does not take over the problem solving of the adopter. The change agent, nevertheless, does provide guidance.

Change agents must consider local resources and expertise important in solving the problem or filling the need. The supposed advantage of this model is that the adopter will not only accept the innovation but will also internalize it. The adopter should view the change as a free choice in response to a specific need (Morrish, 1976). This model is very important to keep in mind in working with faculty members.

A second model of the change process, as described by Rogers (1971), is the social interaction model. Researchers have concluded that an individual's decision about an innovation is not an instantaneous act. Rather it is a process that occurs over time and consists of a series of actions. This model proposes that individuals go through five stages in considering the adoption of a new idea.

Awareness.
The individual first learns of the existence of an innovation at this stage but lacks complete information about it (Rogers, 1971). This awareness of the existence of an innovation comes not as the result of a need. Instead, awareness creates the need (Morrish, 1976). This happens all the time through the mass media. Thanks to television we are constantly discovering the need for gadgets and devices that we never knew we needed.

Interest.
The individual develops an interest in the innovation and seeks additional information about it (Rogers, 1971). This stage consists of information-gathering activities and implies some degree of personal commitment.

Evaluation.
The individual makes mental application of the innovation to his or her situation. The individual then decides whether or not to try it (Rogers, 1971). The individual may move quickly into the trial stage.

Trial.
Here the individual applies the innovation on a small scale to determine its utility. For example, a faculty member may invite a librarian into the classroom on a one-time basis. Potential adopters may extend the trial stage over a considerable time.

Adoption.
Finally, the individual may reach the adoption stage. The individual considers the results of the evaluation and trial stages. The individual then decides whether to adopt or reject the innovation. Once an individual adopts the innovation, then the individual uses it continuously on a full scale.

Strategies

Research shows that certain adoption strategies work at different stages of the adoption process. Guba suggested six general groups of adoption strategies: telling, showing, helping, involving, training, and intervening (Guba, cited in Jwaideh, n.d.). They relate more closely to the social interaction model, but also incorporate elements of the problem-solving model.

Telling.
This is simply communication with written or spoken words. It might take the form of newsletters, brochures, speeches, informal conversations, and mass media communications. Evidence suggests that the media play an important role at the awareness and interest stage. Nevertheless, tactics such as using printed materials do little to convince people to try or adopt an innovation. Morrish (1976) reported that in certain sociological studies media and commercial sources first brought news of an innovation. Nevertheless, adopters often required information from friends, colleagues, and professional sources to legitimatize decisions to adopt or reject the innovation.

Showing.
This is communication that involves direct contact with an innovation through observation. This can include demonstrations, slides, and classroom visits. Getting instructors to visit the classroom of another instructor where a librarian presents bibliographic instruction may be a useful technique. All parties need considerable trust and respect for each other.

Helping.
This is direct involvement of the change agent in the affairs of the potential adopter, on the potential adopter's terms. This may take the form of consultation or troubleshooting. Probably the potential adopter must have reached the trial stage before a change agent tries this strategy. Researchers emphasize this technique in the problem-solving model. Change agents must be careful since it is easy to move from helping to intervening. Faculty members, for example, may resent what they can perceive as an intrusion of the librarian into the classroom.

Involving.
This strategy requires participation of the potential adopter. This strategy may include asking an instructor to help solve a particular teaching problem, to talk about how his or her students use the library, or to discuss students' ability to use the library. A librarian, for example, might ask a faculty member who is using bibliographic instruction on a trial basis to explain his or her methods to another faculty member. Through this strategy the first faculty member may become even more committed to the use of bibliographic instruction.

Training.
This strategy consists of familiarizing potential adopters with a proposed new idea. It may involve helping them to increase their skills or to alter their attitudes. Change agents may offer workshops and in-service training. This strategy can include other strategies, such as telling, showing, helping, and involving. Sometimes the instructor being present in the classroom when the librarian offers bibliographic instruction to students results in a certain amount of training.

Intervening.
Intervening is a strategy in which the change agent directly involves himself or herself on his or her terms, rather than the potential adopter's terms. It seldom happens in bibliographic instruction since, in general, librarians lack the influence to use it successfully. It involves mandating certain actions, such as forcing the adoption of specific textbooks. It is a high risk strategy since the backlash can seriously threaten the success of an innovation. Even deans and presidents hesitate to use it since faculty members have a strong resistance to being managed.

Various techniques with these strategies work with different effectiveness. Bringing in an outside expert to lecture on an innovation often is ineffective, particularly if careful preparation does not precede the visit. A visit to another school that has adopted an innovation is often very effective. Our experience with Earlham College has confirmed this.

There is one technique which research shows works at all stages of the adoption process. It is personal contact. House emphasized his conclusion that most innovations are dependent on face-to-face personal contact. He believed that personal contact determines the frequency and occurrence of innovations. Most individuals, he found, adopt innovations through this medium (House, 1974).

This method may be of particular importance to librarians. There are few serious studies of librarian-classroom instructor relations. Nevertheless, Cameron and Messinger (1975) found, "Poor communications is the prime area of difficulty between librarians and faculty" (p. 26). Often faculty members are unaware of library problems and procedures and librarians often are unaware of curriculum developments and needs. Many libraries, concluded these researchers, lack formal methods of informing the faculty members of the services of the library.

Orientation Toward Change

Faculty members, of course, vary in their orientation to change. Gaff and Wilson (1970) surveyed the attitudes of about 1,000 faculty members toward several specific educational changes. From this information they grouped the faculty into thirds. They then compared the one-third high scoring prochange faculty members with the one-third low scoring antichange faculty members.

Gaff and Wilson (1970) found antichange oriented faculty members considered vocational and technical competence the most important educational goal. Antichange faculty members emphasized a subject-matter or teacher orientation. Factual understanding and fundamentals formed the center of their teaching. These faculty members downplayed a significant student role in policy making and academic affairs and out-of-class contact with students. They stressed structured evaluations, such as objective tests and grading on the curve.

The prochange faculty members considered student development as the most important educational goal. These faculty members related coursework to other fields of study. They involved students in making class plans and policy. They favored out-of-class contacts with students. Most important to this study, prochange faculty members used less structured evaluation procedures, such as term papers and essay exams.

Wilson et al. (1975) found the prochange faculty members came more from the lower academic ranks. They found women overrepresented in the group. The antichange faculty members came disproportionately from the senior ranks in the natural sciences and many fields of applied study.

SUMMARY

Faculty, in general, are well known for their resistance to curricular changes. As one wag put it, faculty members are liberal in other peoples' affairs and conservative in their own. Their orientation into faculty culture instills values and attitudes that inhibit them from strongly encouraging their undergraduates to use the library. Suspended judgment, skepticism, and misgivings about nonfaculty characterize their culture.

Nevertheless, researchers have found that faculty members accept those changes they understand. Some faculties, in fact, have adjusted quite well to new role demands (Cross, 1976). A body of literature exists that will help librarians in encouraging faculty members to involve the library more in undergraduate education. To apply information from this literature to specific situations, librarians must consider their local situation. They need to understand both themselves and the culture in which they live. Finally, they must develop plans to tap the reservoir of existing faculty sentiment for change. Through these means, librarians can develop strategies to reduce incrementally the gap between the current practice and the ideal of library integration in undergraduate education.

chapter ten

CONCLUSIONS AND RECOMMENDATIONS

The contradictions and complexities of faculty culture are never more obvious than in the library. An institution's faculty members largely determine both the quality of the library and of its involvement in undergraduate education. Primarily because of the faculty, academic libraries have grown from the modest collections of inaccessible "diversionary" readings of some 150 years ago. Today we have incredibly rich collections that often includes hundreds of thousands, even millions, of items.

Nevertheless, also primarily because of the faculty, we have a considerable discrepancy between the proclaimed and the actual role of the library in undergraduate education. Far from "the heart of the college," a better analogy might be the spleen. Many undergraduates barely know it exists, few know its purpose, and most could live without it.

Why has this occurred? For the answer we need look no further than the incongruous nature of faculty culture. Trained to add to the body of knowledge, most faculty members primarily serve to diffuse it. Faculty members spend most of their time doing that for which graduate school has not prepared them to do—teaching. Their institutions and colleagues provide the most rewards for that which most faculty members do part-time (if at all)—research. A love of learning attracted most of them to the faculty. They, however, must cope with undergraduates frequently more interested in vocational concerns. It is no wonder there is often an underlying sense of stress and strain among faculty members.

Support of the library allows faculty members to reduce some of the dissonance of their culture. Even if one cannot conduct scholarship, one can participate in it through supporting the library. Selection of library books appeases the conscience. It allows faculty members to apply their knowledge—to make discretionary purchases. For many, it has become part of faculty prerogatives.

Having a good library nearby also is a comfort. It adds prestige and status to the institution (and to the individuals within the institution). The library has a certain psychological value to many faculty members aside from any use by either faculty members or students.

On the other hand, the library adds to the anxiety of the faculty. Few faculty members can keep up with the literature in their discipline. Even fewer add significantly to it. Nevertheless, most feel they should do both. Many faculty members feel uneasy, even defensive, when reminded how little undergraduates use or know how to use the library. The library can represent the unfulfilled ideals instilled in faculty members in graduate school. The library contains the books yet unread and awaits books yet unwritten.

Just how and when (and perhaps why) to engage undergraduates in use of the library are mysteries to many faculty members. Few graduate school professors emphasized to prospective faculty members that the library should be important in undergraduate education. Few faculty members have discussed with their mentors or colleagues how to involve indifferent, perhaps even reluctant, undergraduates in using the library.

Bibliographic instruction in higher education has a long history (Hardesty, Schmitt, & Tucker, 1986). Nevertheless, we found only at Earlham College strong evidence of cooperative projects among faculty members to develop progressive and sequential library assignments. While we found individual faculty members at other institutions who involved undergraduates in use of the library, they seemed isolated within their departments. In our interviews, many of these faculty members expressed an awareness of their isolation.

Seldom outside of Earlham College did we find any excitement or enthusiasm, sense of imagination or creativity, or even a strong sense of purpose or accomplishment from faculty members about the library's involvement in their teaching. Too often we found library assignments they described as unimaginative and predictable. Most students could satisfy them by descriptive compilations of information not requiring application of higher-order cognitive skills.

We seldom met hostility towards the library and librarians from the faculty members (but we did meet it). Nevertheless, we did find considerable indifference, passivity, and inertia toward the library. In the face of these responses, we left many interviews wondering why we had chosen the academic library profession. The thought that intensive, inspired, and imaginative use of the library should be part of undergraduate education is not part of faculty culture.

In fact, a few faculty members we interviewed even suggested that undergraduate use of the library is not a good idea. Perhaps, they stated, undergraduates cannot handle all that information. They might read something inappropriate or unsuitable. They cannot understand the language.

The library can be a crutch. We suspect, worst of all in the eyes of a few faculty members, undergraduates might read something unfamiliar or disagreeable to the teacher. Considering all the effort and the risks, we found many faculty members who decided it is simply better not to have undergraduates use the library.

The resolution of this problem, however, is not for us nor our library colleagues to point fingers at faculty members. We believe, based on our study, despite their strong graduate school socialization and disciplinary orientation, local circumstances and individuals can influence faculty members. In fact, without the catalyst of librarians we conclude that even fewer faculty members would engage their undergraduates in use of the library. Even at Earlham, we suspect, because of the information we gained from our interviews, enthusiasm for the library would wane among some professors without the stimulus of the librarians. Therefore, to more fully incorporate the library into undergraduate education, librarians need to develop a better understanding of the faculty and their culture. We hope through this study that we have added to this understanding.

Faculty members do have considerable knowledge in their subject areas. They should know how to evaluate the books and journals in their areas. Despite their lack of formal training, faculty members have much to add from their classroom teaching experience to the educational process. Faculty members give students the assignments and weigh the results. The faculty members, not librarians, predominately determine the content of courses and the nature of the curriculum. Finally, we must remember, faculty members, not administrators, students, alumni, nor trustees are the strongest supporters of the library.

Therefore, if librarians are to strengthen the role of the library in undergraduate education, they must engage the faculty in the process. Librarians should take advantage of the strengths of faculty members. Librarians must understand and appreciate the apprehensions, the sensibilities, and the shortcomings of faculty members.

Faculty members often find themselves isolated in their classrooms. Seldom do they discuss their teaching with their colleagues. Librarians can offer a nonevaluative (and a nonthreatening) ear. Faculty members tend to view library use from their own experiences. Librarians often are more aware of how students perceive and use the library. Faculty members usually focus on their specialties. Librarians can offer an interdisciplinary perspective. Faculty members emphasize content. Librarians emphasize process. Scholarly curiosity can be infinite. Often faculty members find it hard to establish book selection priorities and limits. Available resources are finite. Most librarians understand the need to establish priorities and limits in the acquisition of knowledge.

Both librarians and faculty have credible areas of specialization and viable perspectives. Both parties can more effectively serve the educational needs of undergraduates when they share their knowledge. Ernest Boyer (1987), in his recent book *College: The Undergraduate Experience in America,* wrote:

> For the library to become a central learning resource on the campus, we need, above all, liberally educated librarians, professionals who understand and are interested in undergraduate education, who are involved in educational matters, and who can open the stacks to students, create browsing rooms, reform the reserve book system, help distribute books throughout campus, and expand holdings in ways that enrich the undergraduate experience. (p. 165)

We commend and share many of his recommendations. We, however, believe Boyer overlooked the possibility that librarians can make their most significant contribution through working directly with faculty members.

Sometimes librarians behave as if they are rearranging the deck chairs on the Titanic. They cannot do much about the direction of the ship but at least they are doing something. Perhaps they spend too much time on displays, browsing rooms, special collections, and even computer projects. The real need in undergraduate education (and the more difficult challenge) is for librarians to engage faculty members in imaginative and resourceful ways to involve undergraduates in use of the library. This may involve a rethinking of the whole undergraduate educational enterprise— perhaps a task not unlike trying to change the direction of the Titanic. Nevertheless, we think the results will justify the effort.

In 1868 John Stuart Mills defined the baccalaureate degree as "the mastery of the body of knowledge that mankind had achieved up to that time" (quoted by Boyer, 1975, p. 20). For at least the past 80 years the undergraduate degree has meant four years of study. Knowledge during that time has increased multifold. Today many institutions offer undergraduates choices among hundreds of fields of study and thousands of courses. We agree with Boyer that students today could not meet Mills' criteria even with 20 years of undergraduate study (Boyer, 1975). In fact, the growing mass of knowledge convinces us that undergraduates today could not master the body of knowledge of *even one discipline* even if we doubled or tripled the length of undergraduate study.

What then is the answer? We should quit behaving as if the principal aim of undergraduate study is to fill the minds of undergraduates with all the knowledge they will ever need over their lifetimes. Four years is hardly time to do more than a cursory sampling of existing knowledge. We need to quit believing that the highest (and only) purpose of undergraduate education is to clone more individuals in the faculty image.

The siren of specialization is tempting but we must wonder at what sacrifice is it sought at the undergraduate level. Do faculty members offer their highly specialized courses because every undergraduate needs an understanding of ———— (each of us could fill in the blank with an appropriate course in a narrow subspecialty from even a brief examination of an undergraduate catalog)? Or, are these courses offered because faculty members find such courses, based on their graduate school orientation, more exciting, more intellectually stimulating, and more related to the specialty around which their careers centers than broader focused courses?

None of these reasons are inherently wrong. Faculty members, however, should temper these motivations with an examination of undergraduate education. What do undergraduates need to become productive members of society? What can and should be accomplished in four short undergraduate years? We believe more faculty members need to get their fulfillment from the individual development of undergraduates.

Undergraduate education should provide the opportunity to develop an understanding of our cultural heritage and the perspectives offered by the various disciplines. It should provide an opportunity for undergraduates to explore some topics in depth and to develop an appreciation for the creation of knowledge. We believe the topics are less important than the development of analytical and evaluative cognitive skills. Undergraduates should develop an understanding and appreciation for both interpretation and experimentation as sources of knowledge.

In undergraduate education, we need to prepare students for the year after they graduate, and the year after that, and the rest of their lives. We need to prepare students for the time when we are not available to guide them. They must develop the ability to locate, analyze, and evaluate knowledge since it will continually expand during their lifetimes. All this leads to the library. We agree with S. K. Baily (1976), who wrote:

> Both the past and the intellectual stimulate for our future live predominantly and supremely in our libraries. Perhaps the most exalted responsibility of professors and literary circles is to guide people to those books and articles that will help them in the world of their free selves to discover or rediscover who they are and what they have the chance of becoming. (p. 73)

Perhaps the highest responsibility of undergraduate faculty members and librarians is to develop in students the ability to make good use of the library.

ATTITUDE SCALE CHARACTERISTICS

INTRODUCTION

We provide this technical information on the attitude scale's psychometric characteristics to give the reader an understanding of its strengths and limitations. Since we encourage replication of this study, we want potential users to have enough information to make informed judgments about its use. The terminology used, more frequently found in psychology than in library literature, may be unfamiliar to the reader. We, however, explain the significance of this information and refer the reader to additional sources for further explanations. In particular, for further information on the development of the attitude scale see Hardesty (1982).

RELIABILITY

Tests-retests and Equivalent Forms

A reliable measure provides consistent and stable evidence of the characteristics measured (Anderson, Ball, Murphy, & Associates, 1976). For example, we might use a scale several times to measure an attitude. We then determine if the scores are similar (Shaw & Wright, 1967). In addition to the test-retest procedure, we might use equivalent-forms of a test or scale to measure reliability. While at first glance these methods seem appealing, several researchers have noted their limitations.

Several factors unrelated to the scale may cause different responses from one time to another. Memory, anxiety, and fatigue all may result in different scores. Large but misleading correlations among the test scores can result. Retesting frequently provides unacceptable estimates of reliability (Joint Committee, 1974). Obviously, in this study, as with most studies, practical limitations entered the picture. We doubt we could persuade faculty members to respond several times to the attitude scale.

Using the equivalent-form method we could ask individuals to respond to one form of a scale and then to an equivalent form. This method only

TABLE A.1
Reliability, Standard Deviation, and Standard Error of Measurement by Institution

	Earlham	Evansville	Purdue	Wabash	Total
Reliability	.76	.77	.77	.70	.79
Standard Deviation	16.2	16.7	17.3	13.8	17.4
Standard Error of Measurement	7.9	8.0	8.3	7.5	8.0

partially avoids some of the problems of the retest-test method. This method has a more crucial limitation. Seldom can researchers locate or create two interchangeable measures of the same attitudes.

Internal Reliability

Coefficient Alpha.
We can look at reliability in other ways. For example, we can consider internal consistency. That is, do each of the statements measure some part of the same attitude? We can determine estimates of internal consistency by dividing a scale in half and computing the reliability coefficient using the scores from the halves. The scores, however, will vary depending on the division of the items (Nunnally, 1978). To overcome this problem, Kuder and Richardson developed a method that provides a coefficient resulting from split-half coefficients of all possible divisions of a test (Kuder & Richardson, 1937). Cronbach then developed a generalized formula for multiple-scored tests, such as Likert scales, known as the coefficient alpha (Cronbach, 1951).

Coefficient alpha provides a good reliability measure since the major source of measurement error results from the sampling of content (Nunnally, 1978). It also serves as a measure of scale homogeneity (Kerlinger, 1973). We determined the internal reliability of the LEAS through the RELIABILITY subprogram of version 8.1 of the *Statistical Package for the Social Sciences* (SPSS) (Nie, Hadlai, Jenkins, Steinbrenner, & Bent, 1975). For the 234 respondents to the field test, the LEAS had a coefficient alpha of .79 (see Table A.1).

Strong internal consistency helps psychological interpretation of the test. As Cronbach (1951), however, pointed out, we can interpret a scale without factorial similarity of all its items. A large proportion of the test variance must be attributable to the principal factor running through the scale. This detail relates to the discussions of factor analysis. The overall coefficient alpha yields useful information about the understanding of any subtests or factors (Cronbach, 1951).

Several extraneous factors, such as test length and response bias, may influence the reliability score. Nevertheless, we argue these factors did not exert a significant influence in this study. First, with a very low item-correlation, an extremely large number of items would be necessary to gain an acceptable level of reliability. Nunnally (1978) pointed out that with a 40-item test with a reliability of .20 that it would require 640 items to reach a reliability of .80. After a review of the measures reported in recent editions of *Mental Measurements Yearbook,* we concluded the LEAS is not a lengthy scale.

What is a satisfactory level of reliability? Nunnally (1978) recommended that in the early stages of research on predictor tests or hypothesized measures of a construct that reliability of .70 or higher is enough. He argued that for basic research increasing reliabilities beyond .80 usually wasted time and money. Therefore, we consider the coefficient alpha of .79 adequate for this scale. That is, it has enough reliability to help us understand the attitudes of various groups of faculty members. As shown in the following discussion, it has limitations when applied to decisions about individuals.

Response Bias.
Response bias may refer to a particular response set. Respondents may tend to agree or disagree with all items, regardless of their content (Kerlinger, 1973). "Social desirability" also may influence their decisions. They try to express only what they consider "socially desirable" attitudes. Through examination of the responses to each item, we found no evidence of any particular response bias to this scale (see Table A.2). If a response bias existed, we would expect consistent responses on the same side of the neutral point for all items. We also might find consistent disagreement with "socially undesirable" items or vice versa. The interviewed faculty members expressed a full range of both positive and negative attitudes, and the surveyed faculty members responded similarly.

Standard Error of Measurement.
The standard error of measurement is the estimated standard deviation of scores if an individual responded to many tests sampling the same domain. For this scale it is eight points (see Table A.1). The *Standards for Educational and Psychological Testing* recommended reporting this score. It enables "test users to judge whether scores are sufficiently accurate for the intended use of the test" (Committee to Develop Standards, 1985, p. 20). While often misinterpreted (Dudek, 1979), the standard error of measurement shows, along with the reliability coefficient, a confidence interval around the estimated true score (Nunnally, 1978). For example, an individual in this study with a scale score of 155 would have an estimated true score of

TABLE A.2
Library Educational Attitude Scale Summary Statistics

Statements	Responses			
	Positive	Negative	Undecided	Nonresponses
1	34.6%	59.4%	4.3%	1.7%
2	87.1	11.5	.9	.4
3	85.5	12.0	2.1	.4
4	91.4	4.7	3.8	0
5	82.5	12.9	4.7	0
6	45.7	46.9	6.4	.9
7	14.6	81.2	3.4	.9
8	83.8	10.6	4.7	.9
9	99.1	.4	.4	0
10	92.3	5.5	1.7	.4
11	58.2	30.4	11.5	0
12	65.4	23.1	11.5	0
13	53.0	38.0	8.1	.9
14	50.4	38.9	10.7	0
15	45.3	29.9	24.4	.4
16	90.1	6.0	2.1	1.7
17	38.4	53.8	6.0	1.7
18	62.3	26.5	9.0	2.1
19	16.7	72.7	10.3	.4
20	74.4	8.5	16.2	.9
21	61.1	32.9	5.6	.4
22	57.3	32.0	10.7	0
23	90.6	6.5	3.0	0
24	47.1	28.2	23.1	1.7
25	35.9	56.1	8.1	0
26	93.2	3.9	2.6	.4
27	51.3	38.9	9.4	.4
28	67.2	18.8	11.5	2.6
29	51.7	39.3	8.1	.9
30	47.8	34.6	14.5	3.0

Note. Items 1, 2, 3, 5, 10, 13, 15, 17, 19, 24, 25, 27, 28, 29, and 30 are negative statements.

152. The 95 percent confidence level ranges from about 136 to 168 (see Nunnally, 1978, pp. 236–242, for a more complete discussion). The standard error of measurement reminds us of the outward bias in both directions of scores from a test or scale. This bias creates fewer problems in basic research than in applied work. Nevertheless, the reader should use this scale only with an understanding that the scores of individuals can vary within these parameters. Again, for expected uses of this attitude scale, we find the standard error of measurement acceptable.

Item-Analysis.

The domain-sampling model serves as a major part of the theory of reliability. That is, we assume each test is a random sample of items from an attitude domain (Nunnally, 1978). This theory argues for test homogeneity, manifested in the average correlation among items and in the pattern of item-total correlations. Item-analysis, as used in this study, consisted of examining the relationship between scores on individual items to the total scale score. To avoid a deceptively high correlation through self-correlation, we removed the score of each item from the total attitude scale score (Nunnally, 1978). For scale development purposes, the returned scales exceeded the minimum of five per item recommended by Nunnally (1978). In fact, the number of responses approached his suggested rule of thumb of ten responses per item for item analysis.

To produce a homogeneous scale, we should reject those items with low correlations with the total score. According to Nunnally's criteria, a 30-item scale with a coefficient alpha of .79 should be relatively homogeneous. Examination of the item-total correlation patterns (see Table A.3) and factor analysis both supported this conclusion.

Twenty-six of the 30 attitude statements correlated positively (when re-coded) at the .01 level with the total attitude scale score. Attitude statements 15, 21, 24, and 25 did not meet this criteria. We compared the individual statement scores of the top and bottom quarters of the respondents using the total scale score (one-tailed t-test of significance at the .05 level). We rejected the null hypothesis of no significant differences between the means of the two groups for items 15 and 21. That is, they do have some discriminatory power. We, however, could not find any discriminatory power for items 24 and 25. Nevertheless, even with the t-test results, all four statements remain questionable contributions to the scale. This is particularly true of both statements 15 and 24 because over 20 percent of the respondents chose the undecided response (see Table A-2).

While we seek item consistency, we also seek efficiency. That is, each statement should provide further description of the attitude measured. Highly overlapping items provide little additional understanding of the attitude. Only statements 1 and 17 correlated with each other at more than the .50 level. The other statements correlate within acceptable levels (see Table A.4).

VALIDITY

Validity is the second important psychometric consideration in attitude scale development. It essentially deals with whether or not the scale mea-

TABLE A.3
Library Educational Attitude Scale Item-Total Correlations

Statement	Correlation
1	.58
2	.38
3	.47
4	.46
5	.35
6	.37
7	.21
8	.31
9	.36
10	.41
11	.26
12	.47
13	.22
14	.21
15	.01*
16	.26
17	.54
18	.35
19	.23
20	.21
21	.06*
22	.33
23	.31
24	−.03*
25	.02*
26	.15
27	.38
28	.43
29	.48
30	.20

Note. Negative statements are recoded. Individual items are removed from total score to avoid self-correlation.
*Item not correlated with total score at .01 level.

sures what we claim it measures, that is, library educational attitudes. We can determine validity with less precision than reliability. Nevertheless, we argue this scale meets the requirements of the major types of validity: content validity, criterion-related validity, and construct validity.

Content Validity

Evidence related to content validity shows "the degree to which the sample of items, tasks, or questions on a test are representative of some defined universe or domain of content" (Committee to Develop Standards, 1985, p. 10). Content validity depends largely on using a sensible method of scale construction. We used the scale development procedures outlined earlier to assure content validity: (a) formulation of proper definitions, (b) collection of many attitude statements from a variety of sources, (c) use of judges, and (d) use of pilot and field tests.

In addition, a moderate level of internal consistency among the statements supports the claim of content validity. We should expect the statements to measure something in common (Nunnally, 1978). Both Cronbach (1971) and Nunnally (1978), however, pointed out that internal reliability alone is not an infallible guide to content validity of an instrument. Essentially, Kerlinger (1973) concluded, "Content analysis consists essentially in judgments" (p. 458). Do the items individually or collectively represent the attitude domain in question?

Criterion-related Validity

Evidence applicable to criterion-related validity shows the relationship of scores to outcome criteria (Committee to Develop Standards, 1985). The criterion directly measures the behavior or other characteristics studied. Theorists usually divide criterion-related validity into two groups. Predictive validity relates to measures used for the prediction of future results. Concurrent validity relates to measures employed for diagnosis of existing status (Kerlinger, 1973).

Shaw and Wright (1967) noted that predictive validity is usually most important when one wishes to relate attitudes to actions. In attitude research, however, researchers usually seek to relate attitudes to such variables as education, socioeconomic status, and other attitudes rather than to prediction of future results. We, of course, would like to relate library educational attitudes to particular behaviors of faculty members. Nevertheless, as Shaw and Wright pointed out, very few researchers have confirmed scales by the predictive method because of "the relatively large amount of work required" (p. 56). Therefore, we have concentrated on concurrent validity and leave to additional research the question of predictive validity.

Measures used for classification need concurrent validity (Committee to Develop Standards, 1985). We used compared group scores to prove concurrent validity. Anastasi (1982) described this method as "contrasted groups" (p. 144). Shaw and Wright (1967) called it "known-groups" (p. 563). Anastasi (1982) defined contrasted or known-groups as "distinct groups that have been differentiated through the operation of the multiple demands of daily living" (p. 144). We must distinguish these groups from,

TABLE A.4
Library Educational Attitude Scale Correlation Matrix of Field Test Results

Item	Item 1	Item 2	Item 3	Item 4	Item 5	Item 6	Item 7
1							
2	.26						
3	.32	.29					
4	.35	.31	.22				
5	.28	.39	.21	.35			
6	.20	.06	.21	.24	.00		
7	.17	−.03	.16	.12	.01	.21	
8	.22	.14	.09	.11	.00	.21	.05
9	.21	.25	.25	.39	.23	.21	−.02
10	.32	.27	.41	.25	.33	.13	.03
11	.26	.06	.09	.13	.05	.25	.12
12	.41	.11	.21	.31	.11	.23	.15
13	.24	.22	.16	.05	.14	−.04	.04
14	.18	.10	.11	.24	.22	.13	.07
15	−.07	.12	.03	.02	.04	−.05	−.24
16	.18	.13	.19	.08	.18	.18	.13
17	.58	.14	.25	.30	.20	.25	.18
18	.26	.02	.07	.20	−.06	.25	.14
19	.14	.20	.13	.10	.06	.01	.01
20	.13	.05	.02	.10	.19	.10	.06
21	−.04	−.04	−.02	.03	.00	.12	.04
22	.30	.03	.21	.16	.24	.29	.16
23	.18	.16	.22	.20	.10	.15	.03
24	−.12	.07	.00	−.04	−.01	.01	.00
25	−.01	.10	.04	−.01	.09	−.04	−.16
26	.04	.09	.28	.00	−.04	.24	.09
27	.39	.18	.37	.17	.14	.15	.22
28	.28	.35	.28	.21	.13	.18	.14
29	.43	.21	.27	.33	.28	.22	.21
30	.07	.09	.13	.12	.03	.09	.06

Item	Item 8	Item 9	Item 10	Item 11	Item 12	Item 13	Item 14
9	.21						
10	.06	.28					
11	.43	.19	.09				
12	.32	.21	.18	.24			
13	−.02	.03	.12	−.08	.05		
14	.05	.13	.11	.06	.27	−.05	
15	.03	.04	.03	−.09	−.08	.14	−.14
16	.00	.12	.26	.16	.24	−.07	.10
17	.15	.13	.26	.20	.41	.12	.28
18	.22	.14	.02	.21	.28	.10	.11
19	.05	.04	.17	−.05	.08	−.01	.07
20	.27	.13	.11	.13	.30	.03	.11
21	.17	.13	−.06	.13	.08	−.01	.07
22	.05	.10	.18	.24	.30	−.03	.13

TABLE A.4 (Continued)
Library Educational Attitude Scale Correlation Matrix of Field Test Results

Item	Item 8	Item 9	Item 10	Item 11	Item 12	Item 13	Item 14
23	.15	.23	.22	.20	.30	−.05	.07
24	−.03	.01	−.08	−.23	−.18	.29	−.21
25	.05	−.05	.01	.04	−.18	.01	−.07
26	.19	.19	.15	.22	.12	−.07	−.12
27	.06	.12	.34	.08	.18	.20	.05
28	.08	.10	.21	−.02	.11	.27	.01
29	.01	.08	.23	.07	.29	.14	.26
30	−.03	−.01	.06	−.01	.07	.11	.04
Item	**Item 15**	**Item 16**	**Item 17**	**Item 18**	**Item 19**	**Item 20**	**Item 21**
16	−.03						
17	−.03	.14					
18	.04	.03	.35				
19	.07	.06	.18	.06			
20	.02	.06	.11	.12	−.09		
21	.07	−.02	−.03	.20	−.10	.19	
22	−.05	.19	.19	.14	−.05	.16	.14
23	−.01	.07	.15	.20	−.03	.24	.01
24	.16	−.17	−.11	.02	.26	−.13	−.04
25	.04	−.02	.07	.00	.12	−.11	.05
26	−.02	.21	.02	.05	−.01	.12	.00
27	−.08	.09	.40	.11	.17	−.06	−.11
28	.08	.22	.18	.23	−.05	−.05	.11
29	−.18	.47	.18	.15	.13	−.03	.22
30	.14	.12	.05	.07	.17	.02	.03
Item	**Item 22**	**Item 23**	**Item 24**	**Item 25**	**Item 26**	**Item 27**	**Item 28**
23	.42						
24	−.19	−.12					
25	.01	−.06	.10				
26	−.03	.18	.00	−.09			
27	.11	−.03	−.06	.04	.08		
28	.11	.12	.33	.10	.05	.30	
29	−.22	.13	−.05	.00	−.16	.40	.32
30	.02	.08	.15	.06	.04	.02	.27
Item	**Item 29**						
30	.16						

Note. Negative statements recoded; Level of significance approximately .15 at probability = .01 for n = 234.

for example, groups assigned on a random basis for an experimental treatment.

Researcher have long used group differences to examine both concurrent and construct validity. Indeed, Cronbach and Meehl (1955) cited Thurstone and Chave's pioneer study (1929). These early researchers tested the "Scale for Measuring Attitude Toward the Church" by showing score differences between churchgoers and nonchurchgoers. Cronbach and Meehl pointed out "churchgoing" did not serve as the criterion of the attitude. Failure to find a difference, however, would have questioned the validity of the test. As with the Thurstone and Chave (1929) study, we expected that members of the different groups examined in this study would hold different attitudes.

We asked the judges to provide criterion groups. They clearly selected faculty of small liberal arts colleges as more supportive of the library's role in undergraduate education than faculty of research universities. The judges less clearly defined criterion groups according to discipline and tenure status. Higher education literature, however, provided evidence to hypothesize about the importance of discipline in shaping educational attitudes of faculty (Ladd & Lipset, 1975a).

In addition, library literature provided evidence that Earlham College faculty members would support strongly an active role of the library in undergraduate education (Kennedy, 1970; Farber, 1974b). Therefore, based on the judges responses, a review of the literature, and our experiences, we hypothesized that the Earlham College faculty members would be more positive than faculty members at the other institutions. We hypothesized that the Purdue University biological science undergraduate faculty members would be less positive than the faculty members at the other institutions. We hypothesized that discipline might relate to library educational attitudes. We, however, did not expect other variables included in the study to relate significantly to library educational attitudes.

As shown earlier, we found differences among the average attitude scores among the faculty at the four institutions. The faculty members at Earlham College had a significantly higher average total score than did the other faculty members. The faculty members at Purdue University had a significantly lower average total score than did the other faculty members. We found no differences among the faculty members based on the other academic and demographic variables, including discipline. These findings support the claim of criterion-related validity for this attitude scale.

Construct Validity

What is a construct? In their major article on the topic, Cronbach and Meehl (1955) defined it as "some postulated attribute of people, assumed to be reflected in test performance" (p. 283). In this study, construct validity refers to the validity with which the attitude scale depicts the psychological construct of library educational attitudes. Among the types of validity, construct validity is the most difficult to show and to explain.

Nevertheless, according to Kerlinger (1973), "In a sense, any type of validation is construct validation" (p. 466). Cronbach and Meehl (1955) provided an extensive discussion of several methods of construct validation. We can use much of the evidence of content and criterion-related validity to show construct validity. As with content validity, the procedures used for attitude scale development supports the claim of construct validity. We widely sampled faculty statements, considered judgments of knowledgeable individuals, and analyzed the results of the pilot and field tests. The differences in scale scores among the faculty from different institutions provided evidence of both construct and criterion-related validity. Other evidence supports construct validity. Internal consistency, provided by item-test correlations and coefficient alpha reliability, pertains to construct validity (Cronbach & Meehl, 1955). The moderately high internal consistency displayed by this scale supports claims of construct validity (Nunnally, 1978). Factor analysis also bolstered construct validity claims. It showed that no unusual element, such as responses to one particular item, largely influenced the scale score (Cronbach, 1971).

Few developers of tests and attitude scales provide complete evidence of construct validity. Both Anastasi (1982) and Cronbach and Meehl (1955) criticized claims of construct validity without empirical data. In particular, correlational studies recommended by Cronbach (1971) could strengthen claims of construct validity for this scale. We, however, need other valid and reliable variables with which to correlate the LEAS. Research on the educational attitudes of faculty remains scanty and uncoordinated, as noted by several investigators (Light, 1974; Mangano, 1972; Morstain & Smart, 1976; Wilkerson, 1977). Therefore, while we provide evidence of construct validity, we encourage caution and further research.

SUMMARY

We provide sufficient evidence of reliability and validity for this scale to make it widely useful in furthering the understanding of the library educational attitudes of undergraduate faculty. We carefully constructed it through numerous interviews and pilot and field-tested it among a wide range of faculty. We believe it meets necessary standards for the classification of groups of faculty and to relate their attitudes toward their other characteristics. Further research may refine this scale. Addition or deletion of statements, however, may change its reported psychometric characteristics.

A SCALE TO MEASURE ATTITUDES OF CLASSROOM INSTRUCTORS TOWARD THE ROLE OF THE ACADEMIC LIBRARY IN UNDERGRADUATE EDUCATION*

DIRECTIONS

The academic library is an important part of every college and university. Nevertheless, considerable evidence exists that many undergraduate students neither use nor know how to use the academic library. Also, considerable evidence exists that a large portion of the materials acquired for the academic library is seldom used.

The role of the academic library may be influenced by a number of factors, such as the purpose of the college or university, the size and type of collections available, the accessibility of the collections, the study conditions available, and the attitudes and abilities of students, librarians, administrators and classroom instructors. Many researchers consider classroom instructors to play the dominant role in determining undergraduate student use of the academic library. This scale seeks to identify the attitudes that classroom instructors hold toward the educational role of the academic library at the undergraduate level.

Please read each of the statements carefully and for each one indicate your answers. Your response should reflect your attitude as a result of *your experiences* in teaching *undergraduate students* in *your discipline*.

You should indicate your choice by *circling one* of the seven choices allowing the expression of attitudes from strong agreement to strong disagreement.

Circle AAA,   if you *strongly agree*
Circle AA,   if you *moderately agree*
Circle A,   if you *slightly agree*

---

* © Copyright 1982 by Larry Hardesty.

> Circle U,   if you are *undecided*
> Circle D,   if you *slightly disagree*
> Circle DD,   if you *moderately disagree*
> Circle DDD,   if you *strongly disagree*

Please turn the page for examples of how to indicate your answer.

Example One

Academic librarians should be less concerned with rules and regulations in order to encourage students to use the library.

AAA   AA   Ⓐ   U   D   DD   DDD

If you *agree* with this statement *slightly*, you should circle "A" as shown.

Example Two

It should be the role of the classroom instructor, not librarians, to teach students how to use the library.

AAA   AA   A   U   D   ⒹⒹ   DDD

If you *disagree* with this statement *moderately*, you should circle "DD" as shown.

Make sure that you circle a symbol for each statement. Leave none of the items blank and make only *one* circle for *each item*. In some cases, you may believe you do not know how to judge a statement. When this occurs, please make the best estimate of your attitude you can or circle "U" for undecided. You should not spend more than a few seconds on each item.

PLEASE COMPLETE THE FOLLOWING INFORMATION BEFORE PROCEEDING TO THE FIRST ITEM

1) Name: _____ 2) Institution: _____
3) Rank: _____ Instructor   _____ Assistant Professor
   _____ Associate Professor   _____ Professor
   _____ Other (specify) _____
4) Academic Department: _____
5) Your Highest Degree: _____ Masters   _____ Doctorate   _____ Other
   (specify) _____
6) Institution Awarding your Highest Degree: _____
7) Total Number of Years Teaching at Present Institution: _____

8) Total Number of Years in Higher Education: _____
9) Tenure Status: ____Tenured ____Untenured
10) Sex: ____Male ____Female
11) Age: ____Under 26 ____26–30 ____31–35 ____36–40
    ____41–45 ____46–50 ____51–55 ____56–60
    ____61–65 ____Over 65

PLEASE PROCEED TO THE FIRST ITEM

1. Teaching additional content in my lower-level courses should be more important than spending time teaching my students how to use the library.

    AAA   AA   A   U   D   DD   DDD

2. I should expect only my brightest students to make good use of the library collections.

    AAA   AA   A   U   D   DD   DDD

3. A knowledge of how to use the card catalog should be sufficient familiarity with the library for students to use it for my courses.

    AAA   AA   A   U   D   DD   DDD

4. I should help my students develop the ability to use the literature of my discipline available in the library.

    AAA   AA   A   U   D   DD   DDD

5. Assignments requiring students to use the library demand too much of my time in relation to my other responsibilities.

    AAA   AA   A   U   D   DD   DDD

6. My students should have specific instructions on how to use the library in each course in which I require its use.

    AAA   AA   A   U   D   DD   DDD

7. It should take considerable time for students to master the skills needed to use the library for my courses.

    AAA   AA   A   U   D   DD   DDD

8. Administrators should promote the view that librarians are full partners with me in the educational process.

    AAA   AA   A   U   D   DD   DDD

9. I should be familiar with the range of library resources useful in teaching my students.

   AAA   AA   A   U   D   DD   DDD

10. For students in my courses, the library should be considered primarily as a place to study textbooks, lecture notes, and similar materials.

    AAA   AA   A   U   D   DD   DDD

11. Administrators should take a leadership role in encouraging student use of the library.

    AAA   AA   A   U   D   DD   DDD

12. I should develop an interesting problem or quest to introduce my students to the library.

    AAA   AA   A   U   D   DD   DDD

13. The size of the library collections in my discipline should serve as a measure of how well the library will serve the needs of my students.

    AAA   AA   A   U   D   DD   DDD

14. I should have the main responsibility for ensuring that my students make good use of the library.

    AAA   AA   A   U   D   DD   DDD

15. Librarians should have advanced degrees in other disciplines in addition to a degree in library science if they are to help students use the library.

    AAA   AA   A   U   D   DD   DDD

16. My students should use the library to learn how scholars examine major works and ideas in my discipline.

    AAA   AA   A   U   D   DD   DDD

17. Teaching additional content in my upper-level courses should be more important than spending time teaching my students how to use the library.

    AAA   AA   A   U   D   DD   DDD

18. I should be better prepared to teach students how to make good use of the library.

    AAA   AA   A   U   D   DD   DDD

19. The library should be quiet to encourage my students to use it.

    AAA   AA   A   U   D   DD   DDD

20. I should evaluate the library assignments of my students on the same basis as any other assignments for my courses.

    AAA   AA   A   U   D   DD   DDD

21. The small college library should satisfy the library needs of my undergraduate students just as adequately as the large university library.

    AAA   AA   A   U   D   DD   DDD

22. It should reflect poorly on my department if the library is not heavily used by students in our courses.

    AAA   AA   A   U   D   DD   DDD

23. I should be concerned if the library collection in my discipline is little used.

    AAA   AA   A   U   D   DD   DDD

24. Administrators should ensure small classes to encourage me to require my students to use the library.

    AAA   AA   A   U   D   DD   DDD

25. Student frustration in using the library should be considered a normal part of learning how to use the library.

    AAA   AA   A   U   D   DD   DDD

26. Librarians should help me by teaching my students how to use the library.

    AAA   AA   A   U   D   DD   DDD

27. Students should be able to learn needed library skills in my discipline quickly and independently.

    AAA   AA   A   U   D   DD   DDD

28. Administrators should seek to admit a high proportion of very capable students if they want me to require my students to use the library.

    AAA   AA   A   U   D   DD   DDD

29. I should be able to leave to librarians the responsibility of teaching students how to use the library.

    AAA   AA   A   U   D   DD   DDD

30. Being surrounded by books in the library should have a positive influence on students whether they use them or not.

     AAA   AA   A   U   D   DD   DDD

☐ Please check here if you want a summary of the results of this study.

Please feel free to make any comments concerning this study.

Thank you for your cooperation.

Larry Hardesty
Director of Library Services
Eckerd College
Box 12560
St. Petersburg, FL 33733-2560

REFERENCES

ACRL. (1975). *Books for college libraries* (2nd ed.). Chicago: American Library Association.

ACRL. (1988). *Books for college libraries* (3rd ed.). Chicago: American Library Association.

Ajzen, I., & Fishbein, M. (1977, September). Attitude-behavior relations: A theoretical analysis and review of empirical research. *Psychological Bulletin, 84,* 888–918.

Allport, G. W. (1935). Attitudes. In C. Murchinson (Ed.), *A handbook of social psychology* (pp. 798–844). Worchester, MA: Clark University Press.

Allport, G. W. (1968). The historical background of modern social psychology. In G. Lindzey & E. Aronson (Eds.), *The handbook of social psychology* (2nd ed., Vol. 2, pp. 1–80). Reading, MA: Addison-Wesley.

Altbach, P. G. (1985). Stark realities: The academic profession in the 1980s. In M. J. Finkelstein, (Ed.), *Faculty and faculty issues in colleges and universities* (pp. 13–27). Lexington, MA: Ginn.

American library directory. (1984). (37th ed.). New York: R. R. Bowker.

American library directory. (1986). (39th ed.). New York: R. R. Bowker.

Anastasi, A. (1982). *Psychological testing* (5th ed.). New York: Macmillan.

Anderson, S. B., Ball, S., Murphy, R. T., & Associates. (1976). *Encyclopedia of educational evaluation.* San Francisco: Jossey-Bass.

Astin, A. (1985). *Achieving educational excellence.* San Francisco: Jossey-Bass.

Austin, A. E., & Gamson, Z. F. (1984). *Academic workplace: New demands, heightened tensions* (ASHE-ERIC Higher Education Research Report No. 10). Washington, DC: Association for the Study of Higher Education.

Baily, S. K. (1976). *The purpose of education.* Bloomington, IN: Phi Delta Kappa Education Foundation.

Bany, M. A., & Johnson, L. (1975). *Theory and problems of social psychology.* New York: Macmillan.

Barzun, J. (1968). *The American university.* New York: Harper & Row.

Bayer, A. E. (1973, August). *Teaching faculty in academe: 1972–73* (ACE Research Reports, Vol. 8, No. 2). Washington, DC: Office of Research, American Council on Education.

Becker, H. S., Geer, B., & Hughes, E. C. (1968). *Making the grade: The academic side of college life.* New York: John Wiley.

Benne, K. D., & Birnbaum, M. (1969). Principles of changing. In W. G. Bennis, K. D. Benne, & R. Chin (Eds.), *The planning of change* (2nd ed., pp. 328–335). New York: Holt, Rinehart and Winston.

Bennis, W. G., & Schein E. (1969). Changing organizations. In W. G. Bennis, K. D. Benne, & R. Chin (Eds.), *The planning of change* (2nd ed., pp. 354–365). New York: Holt, Rinehart and Winston.

Bess, J. L. (1982a). Editor's Notes. In J. L. Bess, (Ed.), *Motivating professors to teach effectively: No. 10, new directions for teaching and learning* (pp. 1–6). San Francisco: Jossey-Bass.

Bess, J. L. (1982b). The motivation to teach: Meanings, messages, and morals. In J. L. Bess (Ed.), *Motivating professors to teach effectively: No. 10, new directions for teaching and learning* (pp. 99–107). San Francisco: Jossey-Bass.

Biggs, M. (1981, May/April). Sources of tensions and conflict between librarians and faculty. *Journal of Higher Education, 52,* 182–201.

Blackburn, R. T. (1968). College libraries—Indicated failures: Some reasons—and a possible remedy. *College & Research Libraries, 29,* 171–177.

Blackburn, R. T., Armstrong, E., Conrad, C., Didham, J., & McKune, T. (1976). *Changing practices in undergraduate education.* Berkeley, CA: Carnegie Council on Policy Studies in Higher Education.

Blau, P. M. (1973). *The organization of academic work.* New York: John Wiley.

Bok, D. (1986). *Higher learning.* Cambridge, MA: Harvard University Press.

Bommer, M. (1971). *The development of a management system for effective decision making and planning in a university library.* Unpublished Ph.D. dissertation, University of Pennsylvania, Philadelpha, PA.

Borkowski, C., & MacLeod, M. J. (1979a, May). A faculty response from the University of Pittsburgh. *Journal of Academic Librarianship, 5,* 63–65.

Borkowski, C., & MacLeod, M. J. (1979b). Implications of some recent studies of library use. *Scholarly Publishing, 11,* 3–24.

Borkowski, C., & MacLeod, M. J. (1979c). Report on the Kent study of library use: A University of Pittsburgh reply. *Library Acquisitions: Practice and Theory, 3,* 125–151.

Bowen, H. R., & Schuster, J. H. (1986). *American professors: A national resource imperiled.* New York: Oxford University Press.

Boyer, E. L. (1975). Changing time requirements. In D. W. Vermilye (Ed.), *Learning-centered reform: Current issues in higher education 1975* (pp. 14–22). San Francisco: Jossey-Bass.

Boyer, E. L. (1987). *College: The undergraduate experience in America.* New York: Harper & Row.

Braden, I. A. (1970). *The undergraduate library.* Chicago: American Library Association.

Branscomb, H. (1940). *Teaching with books.* Chicago: Association of American Colleges, American Library Association.

Broadus, R. N. (1980, Fall). Use studies in library collections. *Library Resources & Technical Services, 24,* 317–325.

Brown, R. (1958). *Words and things: An introduction to language.* New York: The Free Press.

Brubacher, J. S., & Rudy, W. (1968). *Higher education in transition: A history of American colleges and universities, 1636–1968* (rev. ed.). New York: Harper & Row.

Bureau of the Census. (1975). *Historical statistics of the United States, colonial times to*

1970, bicentennial edition, part 2. Washington, DC: U.S. Government Printing Office.

Bureau of the Census. (1987). *Statistical abstract of the United States: 1988* (108th ed.). Washington, DC: U.S. Government Printing Office.

Cameron, S. H., & Messinger, K. W. (1975, March). Face the faculty: Prevalent attitudes regarding librarian-faculty relationships. *PLA Bulletin, 30,* 23–26.

Caplow, T., & McGee, R. J. (1958). *The academic marketplace.* New York: Basic Books.

Carlson, R. (1965). *Adoption of educational innovation.* Eugene, OR: The Center for the Advanced Study of Educational Administration.

Carnegie Foundation for the Advancement of Teaching. (1977). *Missions of the college curriculum.* San Francisco: Jossey-Bass.

Cattell, R. B. (1966, April). The scree test for the number of factors. *Multivariate Behavioral Research, 1,* 245–276.

Chickering, A. (1969). *Education and identity.* San Francisco: Jossey-Bass.

Chickering, A., Halliburton, A., Bergquist, W., & Lindquist, J. (1977). *Developing the college curriculum: A handbook for faculty and administrators.* Washington, DC: Council for the Advancement of Small Colleges.

Cialdini, R. B., Petty, R. E., & Cacioppo, J. T. (1981). Attitude and attitude change. In M. R. Rosenzweig & L. W. Porter (Eds.), *Annual review of psychology* (Vol. 32, pp. 357–404). Palo Alto, CA: Annual Reviews.

Clark, B. R. (1987). *The academic life.* Princeton, NJ: The Carnegie Foundation for the Advancement of Teaching.

Clarke, J. A. (1980, November). The ACM periodical bank: A retrospective review. *College & Research Libraries, 41,* 475–482.

Cline, H. F., & Sinnott, L. T. (1981). *Building library collections.* Lexington, MA: Lexington.

College Library Standards Committee, Association of College and Research Libraries. (1986, March). Standards for college libraries, 1986. *College & Research Libraries News, 47,* 189–200.

Collins, J. (1978, Winter). Student library use—A matter of encouragement. *West Virginia Libraries, 31,* 19–21.

Committee to Develop Standards for Educational and Psychological Testing of the American Educational Research Association, the American Psychological Association, and the National Council on Measurement in Education. (1985). *Standards for educational and psychological testing.* Washington, DC: American Psychological Association.

Cook, S. W., & Selltiz, C. A. (1964, July). Multiple-indicator approach to attitude measurement. *Psychological Bulletin, 62,* 36–55.

Corcoran, M., & Clark, S. M. (1984). Professional socialization and contemporary career attitudes of three faculty generations. *Research in Higher Education, 20,* 131–153.

Cronbach, L. J. (1951, September). Coefficient alpha and the internal structure of tests. *Psychometrika, 16,* 297–334.

Cronbach, L. J. (1971). Test validiations. In R. L. Thorndike (Ed.), *Educational Measurement* (2nd ed., pp. 443–507). Washington, DC: American Council on Education.

Cronbach, L. J., & Meehl, P. E. (1955, July). Construct validity in psychological tests. *Psychological Bulletin, 52,* 281–302.

Cross, K. P. (1975). Learner-centered curricula. In D. W. Vermilye (Ed.), *Learner-centered reform: Current issues in higher education 1975* (pp. 54–65). San Francisco: Jossey-Bass.

Cross, K. P. (1976). *Accent on learning.* San Francisco: Jossey-Bass.

Danton, J. P. (1963). *Book selection and collections.* New York: Columbia University Press.

Davis, G. B. (1974). *Management information systems: Conceptual foundations, structure, and development.* New York: McGraw-Hill.

DeGennaro, R. (1977, February). Escalating journal prices: Time to fight back. *American Libraries, 8,* 69–74.

Domas, R. E. (1978). *Correlating the classes of books taken out of and books used within an open-stacks library* (ERIC Document Reproduction Service No. ED 171 282). Syracuse, NY: Syracuse University, School of Education.

Dougherty, R. M., & Blomquist, L. L. (1974). *Improving access to library resources.* Metuchen, NJ: Scarecrow.

Dudek, F. J. (1979, March). The continuing misinterpreation of the standard of error measurement. *Psychological Bulletin, 86,* 335–337.

Eagley, A. H., & Himmelfarb, S. (1978). Attitudes and opinions. In M. R. Rosenzweig (Ed.), *Annual review of psychology* (Vol. 29, pp. 517–554), Palo Alto, CA: Annual Reviews.

Eble, K. E. (1972). *Professors as teachers.* San Francisco: Jossey-Bass.

Eble, K. E. (1983). *The aims of college teaching.* San Francisco: Jossey-Bass.

Eckert, R. E., & Stecklein, J. E. (1961). *Job motivations and satisfactions of college teachers: A study of faculty members in Minnesota colleges.* Washington, DC: U. S. Government Printing Office.

Edwards, A. L. (1957). *Techniques of attitude scale construction.* New York: Appleton-Century-Crofts.

Edwards, A. L., & Kenny, K. C. (1946, February). A comparison of the Thurstone and Likert techniques of attitude scale construction. *Journal of Applied Psychology, 30,* 72–83.

Ekirch, A. A., Jr. (1969). *Ideologies and utopias.* Chicago: Quadrangle Books.

Evans, R. I. (1968). *Resistance to innovation in higher education.* San Francisco: Jossey-Bass.

Farber, E. I. (1974a). College librarians and the university-library syndrome. In E. I. Farber & R. Walling (Eds.), *The academic library: Essays in honor of Guy R. Lyle* (pp. 12–17). Metchen, NJ: Scarecrow.

Farber, E. I. (1974b). Library instruction throughout the curriculum: Earlham College program. In J. Lubans, Jr. (Ed.), *Educating the library user* (pp. 145–162). New York: R. R. Bowker.

Fink, L. D. (1982). *First year on the faculty: A study of 100 beginning college teachers.* Norman, OK: Office of Instructional Services, University of Oklahoma.

Finkelstein, M. J. (1984). *The American academic profession.* Columbus: Ohio State University.

Freedman, M. B., Brown, W., Ralph, N., Shukraft, R., Bloom, M., & Sanford, N. (1979). *Academic culture and faculty development.* Berkeley, CA: Montaigne Press.

Fussler, H. H., & Simon, J. L. (1969). *Patterns in the use of books in large research libraries.* Chicago: University of Chicago Press.

Gaff, J. (1975). *Toward faculty renewal.* San Francisco: Jossey-Bass.

Gaff, J. (1983). *General education today.* San Francisco: Jossey-Bass.

Gaff, J., & Wilson, R. C. (1970, September/October). Moving the faculty. *Change, 2,* 10–12.

Galvin, T. J., & Kent, A. (1977, November 15). Use of a university library collection: Progress report on a Pittsburgh study. *Library Journal, 102,* 2317–2320.

Gardner, R. K. (Ed.). (1974). *Opening day collection* (3rd ed.). Middletown, CT: Choice.

Glines, D. (1973, May). Why innovative schools don't remain innovative. *The Education Digest, 38,* 2–5.

Gorsuch, R. L. (1974). *Factor analysis.* Philadelpha: W. P. Saunders.

Grant, G., & Riesman, D. (1978). *The perpetual dream: Reform and experiment in the American college.* Chicago: University of Chicago Press.

Gross, S. J., & Niman, C. M. (1985, Fall). Attitude-behavior consistency: A review. *Public Opinion Quarterly, 39,* 348–368.

Guba, E. G., & Lincoln, E. S. (1981). *Effective evaluation.* San Francisco: Jossey-Bass.

Gurland, R. H. (1978). Teaching mathematics. In S. M. Cahn (Ed.), *Scholars who teach* (pp. 75–100). Chicago: Nelson-Hall.

Gwinn, N. E. (1980, January). Academic libraries and undergraduate education: The CLR experience. *College & Research Libraries, 41,* 5–16.

Hamburg, M., Clelland, R. C., Bommer, M. R. W., Ramist, L. E., & Whitfield, R. M. (1974). *Library planning and decision-making systems.* Cambridge, MA: MIT Press.

Hardesty, L. (1975). *Student use of the library at Kearney State College.* (ERIC Document Reproduction Service No. ED 104 404). Syracuse, NY: Syracuse University, School of Education.

Hardesty, L. (December 1975/March 1976). The academic library: Unused and unneeded? *Library Scene, 4,* 14–17.

Hardesty, L. (1978). Instructional development in library use education. In C. A. Kirkendall (Ed.), *Improving library instruction: How to teach and how to evaluate* (pp. 11–35). Ann Arbor, MI: Pierian.

Hardesty, L. (1980). *Student use of the library at DePauw University* (ERIC Document Reproduction Service No. ED 187 335). Syracuse, NY: Syracuse University, School of Education.

Hardesty, L. (1981a, Fall). Use of library materials at a small liberal arts college. *Library Research, 3,* 261–283.

Hardesty, L. (1981b). *Use of the library reserve collection at DePauw University.* (ERIC Documents Reproduction Service No. ED 192 734). Syracuse, NY: Syracuse University, School of Education.

Hardesty, L. (1982). *The development of a set of scales to measure the attitudes of classroom instructors toward the undergraduate educational role of the academic library.* Unpublished doctoral dissertation, Indiana University, Bloomington, IN.

Hardesty, L. (1984). The influence of selected variables on attitudes of classroom instructors toward the undergraduate educational role of the academic library. In S. C. Dodson & G. L. Menges (Eds.), *Academic libraries: Myths and realities: Proceedings of the Third National Conference of the Association of College and Research Libraries* (pp. 365–373). Chicago: Association of College and Research Libraries.

Hardesty, L. (1986, March). Book selection for undergraduate libraries: A study of faculty attitudes. *Journal of Academic Librarianship, 12,* 19–25.

Hardesty, L. (1988a). Use of library materials at a small liberal arts college: A replication. *Collection Management, 10,* 61–80.

Hardesty, L. (1988b, September). Recent developments in bibliographic instruction. In *Networking for the future: Developing collections and implementing new technologies: A workshop report* (Appendix III). Atlanta, GA: Southern Education Foundation.

Hardesty, L., & Hastreiter, J. (1988). Mathematics periodicals in selected liberal arts colleges. *Collection Building, 9,* 3–11.

Hardesty, L., & Oltmanns, G. (1989). How many psychology journals are enough? A study of the use of psychology journals by undergraduates. *Serials Librarian, 112,* 133–153.

Hardesty, L., Schmitt, J. P., & Tucker, J. M. (Comps.). (1986). *User instruction in academic libraries: A century of selected readings.* Metuchen, NJ: Scarecrow.

Harris, C. (1977, March). A comparison of issues and in-library use of books. *Aslib Proceedings, 29,* 118–126.

Harry, J., & Goldner, N. S. (1972). The null relationship between teaching and research. *Sociology of Education, 45,* 47–60.

Hawkins, H. (1979). University identity: The teaching and research function. In A. Oleson & J. Voss (Eds.), *The organization of knowledge in modern America, 1860–1920* (pp. 285–312). Baltimore: Johns Hopkins University Press.

Hefferlin, J. B. L. (1971). *The dynamics of academic reform.* San Francisco: Jossey-Bass.

Henry, D. D. (1975). *Challenges past, challenges present: An analysis of American higher education since 1930.* San Francisco: Jossey-Bass.

Hernon, P. (1979). *Use of government publications by social scientists.* Norwood, NJ: Ablex.

Higham, J. (1979). The matrix of specialization. In A. Oleson & J. Voss (Eds.), *The organization of knowledge in modern America, 1860–1920* (pp. 3–18). Baltimore: Johns Hopkins University Press.

Hindle, A., & Buckland, M. K. (1978, Fall). In-library book usage in relation to circulation. *Collection Management, 2,* 265–277.

Hofstadter, R., & Smith, W. (1961). *American higher education: A documentary history.* Chicago: University of Chicago Press.

Hogan, J. D., & Hedgepeth, R. (1983, August). Journal quality: The issue of diversity. *American Psychologist, 38,* 961–962.

1984–1985 Holdings of research libraries in U.S., Canada. (1986, May 21). *Chronicle of Higher Education, 32,* 11.

Holland, J. L. (1966). *The psychology of vocational choice.* Waltham, MA: Blaisdell.

Holland, M. K. (1978). *Educational function of librarians: As perceived by administrators, faculty, and librarians at selected community colleges in California.* Unpublished Ed.D. dissertation. Brigham Young University, Provo, UT.

Holley, E. G. (1976, January). Academic libraries in 1876. *College & Research Libraries, 37,* 15–47.

House, E. (1974). *The politics of educational innovation.* Berkeley, CA: McCutchan.

Hutchins, R. M. (1948, April). The report of the President's commission on higher education. *The Educational Record, 29,* 107–122.

James, W. (1903). The Ph.D. octopus. *Harvard Monthly, 36,* 1–9.

Jencks, C., & Riesman, D. (1968). *The academic revolution.* Garden City, NY: Doubleday.

Joint Committee of the American Psychological Association, the American Educational Research Association, & the National Council on Measurement in Education. (1974). *Standards for educational and psychological tests* (rev. ed.). Washington, DC: American Psychological Association.

Jwaideh, A. R. (n.d.). *Implementation workshop: participation manual* (Mimeographed). Bloomington, IN: UCIDT.

Katz, D., & Kahn, R. L. (1966). *Social psychology of organizations.* New York: John Wiley.

Katz, J. (1962). Personality and interpersonal relations in the college classroom. In N. Sanford (Ed.), *The American college* (pp. 365–396). New York: John Wiley.

Kelman, H. C. (1974, May). Attitudes are alive and well and gainfully employed in the sphere of action. *American Psychologist, 29,* 310–324.

Kennedy, J. R., Jr. (1970, April 15). Integrated library instruction. *Library Journal, 95,* 1450–1453.

Kennedy, J. R., Jr. (1972). A separate course in bibliographic instruction. In S. Lee (Ed.), *Library orientation* (pp. 18–28). Ann Arbor, MI: Pierian.

Kent, A., Montgomery, K. K., Cohen, J., Bulick, S., Sabor, W. N., Flynn, R., & Shirey, D. L. (1978). *A cost-benefit model of some critical library operations in terms of use of materials.* Pittsburgh, PA: University of Pittsburgh.

Kerlinger, F. N. (1973). *Foundations of behavioral research* (2nd ed.). New York: Holt, Rinehart and Winston.

Kim, J., & Mueller, C. W. (1978). *Introduction to factor analysis.* Beverly Hills, CA: Sage.

Kirk, R. E. (1968). *Experimental design: Procedures for the behavioral sciences.* Belmont, CA: Wadsworth, Brooks/Cole.

Kirk, T. G. (1974). Problems in library instruction in four-year colleges. In J. Lubans, Jr. (Ed.), *Educating the library user* (pp. 83–103). New York: R. R. Bowker.

Knapp, P. B. (1958, December). College teaching and the library. *Illinois Libraries, 40,* 828–833.

Knapp, P. B. (1959). *College teaching and the college library* (ACRL Monograph, no. 23). Chicago: American Library Association.

Knapp, P. B. (1961, Fall). The Monteith library project: An experiment in library-college relationship. *College & Research Libraries, 22,* 256–263, 284.

Knapp, P. B. (1965, Fall). The meaning of the Monteith College library program for library education. *Journal of Education for Librarianship, 6,* 117–127.

Knapp, P. B. (1966a). Involving the library in an integrated learning environment. In D. Berge & E. D. Duryea (Eds.), *Libraries and the college climate of learning* (pp. 21–35). Syracuse, NY: Syracuse University.

Knapp, P. B. (1966b). *The Monteith College Library experiment.* New York: Scarecrow.

Knapp, R. H. (1962). Changing functions of the college professor. In N. Sanford (Ed.), *The American College* (pp. 290–311). New York: John Wiley.

Krech, D., & Crutchfield, R. (1948). *Theory and problems of social psychology.* New York: McGraw-Hill.

Kritek, W. J. (1976, Fall). Lessons from the literature on implementation. *Educational Administration Quarterly, 12,* 86–102.

Kuder, G. F., & Richardson, M. W. (1937, September.) The theory of estimation of test reliability. *Psychometrika, 2,* 151–160.

Kuh, D. G., & Whitt, E. (1988). *The invisible tapestry: Culture in American colleges and universities.* Washington, DC: Association for the Study of Higher Education.

Ladd, E. C., Jr. (1979). The work experiences of American college professors: Some data and an argument. In *Faculty career development* (Current Issues in Higher Education No. 2, pp. 3–12). Washington, DC: American Association for Higher Education.

Ladd, E. C., Jr., & Lipset, S. M. (1975a). *The divided academy.* New York: McGraw-Hill.

Ladd, E. C., Jr., & Lipset, S. M. (1975b). What professors think. *Chronicle of Higher Education, 11*(1), 2, 9.

Ladd, E. C., Jr., & Lipset, S. M. (1975c). How professors spend their time. *Chronicle of Higher Education, 11*(5), 2.

Ladd, E C., Jr., & Lipset, S. M. (1976). What do professors like best about their jobs? *Chronicle of Higher Education,* 12(5), 10.

Lancaster, F. W. (1988). *If you want to evaluate your library. . . .* Champaign, IL: University of Illinois, Graduate School of Library and Information Science.

LaPiere, R. T. (1934, December). Attitudes vs. actions. *Social Forces, 13,* 230–237.

Lemon, N. (1973). *Attitudes and their measurement.* London: B. T. Batsford.

Levine, A. (1978). *Handbook on undergraduate curriculum.* San Francisco: Jossey-Bass.

Levine, A., & Weingart, J. (1973). *Reform of undergraduate education.* San Francisco: Jossey-Bass.

Light, D., Jr. (1974, Winter). Introduction: The sociology of the academic professions. *Sociology of Education, 47,* 2–28.

Likert, R. (1932). A technique for the measurement of attitudes. *Archives of Psychology,* No. 140.

Lindgren, J. (1978). Seeking a useful tradition for library user instruction in the college library. In J. Lubans, Jr. (Ed.), *Progress in educating the library user* (pp. 71–91). New York: R. R. Bowker.

Link, A. S. (1955). *American epoch.* New York: Alfred A. Knopf.

Lipset, S. M., & Ladd, E. C., Jr. (1985). The changing social conditions of American academics. In M. J. Finkelstein (Ed.), *Faculty and faculty issues in college and universities* (pp. 28–43). Lexington, MA: Ginn.

Liska, A. E. (1974, April). Emergent issues in the attitude-behavior consistency controversy. *American Sociological Review, 39,* 261–272.

Lyle, G. R. (1963). *The president, the professor, and the college library.* New York: H. W. Wilson.

Lyle, G. R. (1974). *The administration of the college library* (4th ed.). New York: H. W. Wilson.

Mangano, R. M. (1972). *A q-analysis of the educational belief patterns of university faculty members.* Unpublished Ph.D. dissertation, Southern Illinois University, Carbondale, IL.

Marchant, M. P. (1969, September 1). Faculty-library conflict. *Library Journal, 94,* 2886–2889.

Martin, W. B. (1968). *Conformity.* San Francisco: Jossey-Bass.

Mayhew, L. B. (1962). *The smaller liberal arts college.* New York: The Center for Applied Research in Education.

Mayhew, L. B., & Ford, P. J. (1971). *Changing the curriculum.* San Francisco: Jossey-Bass.

McClelland, D. C. (1973). Testing for competence rather than for "intelligence." *American Psychologist, 28,* 1–14.

McGrath, W. C. (1971, July). Correlating the subject of books taken out of and books used within an open-stack library. *College & Research Libraries, 32,* 280–285.

McGuire, W. J. (1969). The nature of attitudes and attitude change. In G. Lindzey & E. Aronson (Eds.), *Handbook of social psychology* (2nd ed., Vol. 3, pp. 136–314). Reading, MA: Addison-Wesley.

McKeachie, W. J. (1962). Procedures and techniques of teaching: A survey of experimental studies. In N. Sanford (Ed.), *The American college* (pp. 312–364). New York: John Wiley.

McNiff, P. J., & members of the Harvard Library staff. (1953). *Catalogue of the Lamont Library, Harvard College.* Cambridge, MA: Harvard University Press.

Merrill, M. (1979). *Regular and irregular library use by faculty members at three universities.* Unpublished Ph.D. dissertation, University of Pittsburgh, PA.

Miles, M. B. (1964). Innovation in education: Some generalizations. In M. B. Miles (Ed.), *Innovation in education* (pp. 631–662). Bureau of Publications, Teachers College, Columbia University, New York.

Morrish, I. (1976). *Aspects of educational change.* New York: John Wiley.

Morstain, B., & Smart, J. C. (1976, December). Educational orientations of faculty: Assessing a personality model of the academic professions. *Psychological Reports, 39,* 1199–1211.

Morton, H. C., & Price, A. J. (1986, Summer). Views on publications, computers, libraries. *Scholarly Communication, 5,* 1–16.

National Enquiry into Scholarly Communications. (1979). *Scholarly communications.* Baltimore: Johns Hopkins University Press.

Newcomb, T. M. (1966). On the definition of attitude. In M. Jahoda & N. Warren (Eds.), *Attitudes, selected readings* (pp. 22–25). Baltimore: Penguin Books.

Newman, F. (1985). *Higher education and the American resurgence.* Princeton, NJ: Carnegie Foundation for the Advancement of Teaching.

Nie, N. H., Hadlai, C. H., Jenkins, J. G., Steinbrenner, K., & Bent, D. H. (1975). *SPSS: Statistical package for the social sciences* (2nd ed.). New York: McGraw-Hill.

Nunnally, J. C. (1978). *Psychometric theory* (2nd ed.). New York: McGraw-Hill.

Oberg, L. R., Schleiter, M. K., & Van Houten, M. (1989, March). Faculty perceptions of librarians at Albion College: Status, role, contribution, and contacts. *College & Research Libraries, 50,* 215–230.

Oleson, A., & Voss, J. (1979). *The organization of knowledge in modern America, 1860–1920.* Baltimore: Johns Hopkins University Press.

Oppenheim, A. N. (1966). *Questionnaire design and attitude measurement.* New York: Basic Books.

Orlosky, D., & Smith, B. O. (1972, March). Educational change: Its origins and characteristics. *Phi Delta Kappan, 53,* 412–414.

Osgood, C. E., Suci, G. J., & Tannebaum, P. H. (1970). Attitude measurement. In G. F. Summers (Ed.), *Attitude measurement* (pp. 227–234). Chicago: Rand McNally.

Palmatier, L. L. (1975, Spring). How teachers can innovate and still keep their jobs. *Journal of Teacher Education, 26,* 60–62.

Parsons, T., & Platt, G. M. (1975). *The American university.* Cambridge, MA: Harvard University Press.

Project on Redefining the Meaning and Purpose of Baccalaureate Degrees. (1985). *Integrity in the college curriculum.* Washington, DC: Association of American Colleges.

Radnor, M., Feller, R., & Rogers, E. (1978). *The diffusion of innovation.* Evanston, IL: Center for the Interdisciplinary Study of Science and Technology, Northwestern University, Evanston, IL.

Regan, D. T., & Fazio, R. (1977, January). On the consistency between attitudes and behavior: Look to the method of attitude formation. *Journal of Experimental Social Psychology, 13,* 28–45.

Rich, H.E., & Jolicoeur, P. M. (1978, November). Faculty role perceptions and preferences in the seventies. *Sociology of Work and Occupations, 5,* 423–445.

Riesman, D. (1975). Educational reform at Harvard College: Meritocracy and its adversaries. In S. M. Lipset & D. Riesman (Eds.), *Education and politics at Harvard* (pp. 281–392). New York: McGraw-Hill.

Riesman, D. (1980). *On higher education.* San Francisco: Jossey-Bass.

Riesman, D., Gusfield, J., & Gamson, Z. (1971). *Academic values and mass education: The early years of Oakland and Monteith.* Garden City, NY: Anchor Books; Doubleday.

Riley, G. (1984). Myths and realities: The college viewpoint. In S. C. Dodson & G. L. Menges (Eds.), *Academic libraries: Myths and realities* (pp. 12–14). Chicago: Association of College and Research Libraries.

Rogers, E. M. (1971). *Communication of innovation.* New York: The Free Press.

Rokeach, M. (1968). *Beliefs, attitudes, and values: A theory of organization and change.* San Francisco: Jossey-Bass.

Romey, B. (1977, November/December). Radical innovation in a conventional framework. *Journal of Higher Education, 48,* 680–697.

Rudolph, F. (1962). *The American college and university.* New York: Knopf.

Rudolph, F. (1977). *Curriculum: A history of the American undergraduate course of study since 1636.* San Francisco: Jossey-Bass.

Rummell, R. J. (1970). *Applied factor analysis.* Evanston, IL: Northwestern University Press.

Rummell, R. J. (1972). *The dimensions of nations.* Beverly Hills, CA: Sage.

Sanford, N. (1962). Higher education as a social problem. In N. Sanford (Ed.), *The American college* (pp. 10–30). New York: Wiley.

Saunders, S. (1982, Winter). Student reliance on faculty guidance in the selection of reading materials: The use of core collections. *Collection Management, 4*, 9–23.

Schad, J. G. (1979, May). Missing the brass ring in the iron city. *Journal of Academic Librarianship, 5*, 60–63.

Schein, E. H., & Bennis, W. G. (1965). *Personal and organizational change through group methods: The laboratory approach.* New York: John Wiley.

Schmidt, G. P. (1957). *The liberal arts college: A chapter in American cultural history.* New Brunswick, NJ: Rutgers University Press.

Schmitt, J. P., & Saunders, S. (1983, September). An assessment of *Choice* as a tool for selection. *College & Research Libraries, 44*, 375–380.

Seiler, L. H., & Hough, R. L. (1970). Empirical comparison of the Thurstone and Likert techniques. In G. F. Summers (Ed.), *Attitude measurement* (pp. 159–173). Chicago: Rand McNally.

Seldin, P. (1987). Research findings on causes of academic stress. In P. Seldin (Ed.), *Coping with faculty stress* (pp. 13–21). San Francisco: Jossey-Bass.

Shaw, C. B. (1931). *A list of books for college libraries* (2nd ed.). Chicago: American Library Association.

Shaw, M. E., & Wright, J. M. (1967). *Scales for the measurement of attitude.* New York: McGraw-Hill.

Sheridan, J. (1979). *In-library and recorded book circulation at Knox College.* Unpublished manuscript.

Sherif, M., & Sherif, C. W. (1969). *Social psychology.* New York: Harper & Row.

Shils, E. (1979). The order of learning in the United States: The ascendancy of the university. In A. Oleson & J. Voss (Eds.), *The organization of knowledge in modern America, 1860–1920* (pp. 19–47). Baltimore: Johns Hopkins University Press.

Shulman, C. H. (1979). *Old expectations, new realities: The academic profession revisited.* Washington, DC: American Association for Higher Education.

Sloan, D. (1971, December). Harmony, chaos, and consensus: The American college curriculum. *Teachers College Record, 73*, 221–251.

Stark, J. S., & Morstain, B. R. (1978, September/October). Educational orientations of faculty in liberal arts colleges. *Journal of Higher Education, 49*, 420–437.

Stephenson, W. K. (1980). Library instruction—The best road to development for faculty, librarians and students. In N. Z. Williams & J. T. Tsukamoto (Eds.), *Library instruction and faculty development: Growth opportunities in the academic community* (pp. 81–84). Ann Arbor, MI: Pierian.

Stewart, B. (1975, September). Periodicals and the liberal arts college library. *College & Research Libraries, 36*, 371–378.

Stewart, C. J., & Cash, W. B. (1974). *Interviewing principles and practices.* Dubuque, IA: Wm. C. Brown.

Stockard, J., Griffin, M. P., & Coblyn, C. (1978). Document exposure counts in three academic libraries: Circulation and in-library use. In C. Chen (Ed.), *Quantitative measurement and dynamic library service* (pp. 136–147). Phoenix, AZ: Oryx.

Study Group on the Conditions of Excellence in American Higher Education. (1984). *Involvement in learning: Realizing the potential of American higher education.* Washington, DC: U. S. Government Printing Office.

Summers, G. F. (1970). Introduction. In G. F. Summers (Ed.), *Attitude measurement* (pp. 1–20).Chicago: Rand McNally.

Thurstone, L., & Chave, E. J. (1929). *The measurement of attitude: A psychophysical method and some experiments with a scale for measuring attitude toward church.* Chicago: University of Chicago Press.

Trochim, M. K. (1981). Measuring academic library use: The ACM model. *The ALA Yearbook, 1981.* Chicago: American Library Association.

Trow, M., & Fulton, O. (1975). Research activity in American higher education. In M. Trow (Ed.), *Teachers and students: Aspects of American higher education* (pp. 39–83). Carnegie Commission on Higher Education. New York: McGraw-Hill.

Tuckman, H. P. (1976). *Publication, teaching and the academic reward structure.* Lexington, MA: Lexington Books.

Undergraduate library shelf list (rev. ed.). (1964). Ann Arbor, MI: University Microfilms.

Veysey, L. (1965). *The emergence of the American university.* Chicago: University of Chicago Press.

Veysey, L. (1973). Stability and experiment in American undergraduate curriculum. In C. Keysen (Ed.), *Content and context: Essays on college education* (pp. 1–63). New York: McGraw-Hill.

Voigt, M. J. (1979, May). Circulation studies cannot reflect research use. *Journal of Academic Librarianship, 5,* 66.

Voigt, M. J., & Treyz, J. H. (1967). *Books for college libraries.* Chicago: American Library Association.

Voluntary support for education, 1982–83. (1984). New York: Council for Financial Aid to Education.

Wagman, F. H. (1956, March). Library service to undergraduate college students: The case for the separate undergraduate library. *College & Research Libraries, 17,* 150–155.

Watson, G. (1969). Resistance to change. In W. G. Bennis, K. D. Benne, & R. Chin (Eds.), *The planning of change* (2nd ed., pp. 488–498). New York: Holt, Rinehart and Winston.

Weintraub, K. J. (1980, January). The humanistic scholar and the library. *Library Quarterly, 50,* 22–39.

Whorf, B. L. (1956). *Language, thought, and reality* (J. B. Carroll, Ed.). Cambridge, MA: Technology Press of MIT.

Wilkerson, L. (1977). *University teaching: A study of faculty attitudes.* Unpublished Ed.D. dissertation, University of Massachusetts, Amherst, MA.

Wilkinson, B. R. (1971, May 1). A screaming success as study halls. *Library Journal, 96,* 1567–1571.

Willie, R., & Stecklein, J. E. (1982). A three-decade comparison of college faculty characteristics, satisfactions, activities, and attributes. *Research In Higher Education, 1,* 81–93.

Wilson, L. (1942). *The academic man.* London: Oxford University Press.

Wilson, L. (1979). *American academics then and now.* New York: Oxford University Press.

Wilson, L. R., Lowell, M. H., & Reed, S. R. (1951). *The Library in college instruction.* New York: H. W. Wilson.

Wilson, R., Gaff, J. G., Dienst, E. R., Wood, L., & Bavry, J. L. (1975). *College professors and their impact on students.* New York: Wiley.

Woodburne, L. S. (1958). *Principles of college and university administration.* Stanford, CA: Stanford University Press.

Woods, W. E. (1965). *Factors influencing student library use: An analysis of studies (1930–1964).* Unpublished M.A. thesis, University of Chicago, IL.

Young, A. P. (1974). Research on library-use education: A review essay. In J. Lubans, Jr. (Ed.), *Educating the library user* (pp. 1–15). New York: R. R. Bowker.

AUTHOR INDEX

SUBJECT INDEX